new CALENDAR graphics

PIE
BOOKS

new CALENDAR graphics

PIE BOOKS
2-32-4, Minami-Otsuka, Toshima-ku,
Tokyo 170-0005 Japan
Phone: +81-3-5395-4811
Fax: +81-3-5395-4812
e-mail: editor@piebooks.com
sales@piebooks.com
http://www.piebooks.com/

ISBN4-89444-257-4 C3070

Printed in Japan

Contents

序 文

書店や雑貨店の店頭がカレンダーで賑わう年末、本書の企画はスタートしました。「デザイン性はもちろん、バリエーションが豊富な作品集にしたい」。そんな編集目標を掲げ、作品収集の日々が続きました。毎日のように国内外のクリエイターから届く、個性溢れる作品。その梱包を解き、中身をあらためる作業は本当に楽しく、時には仕事を忘れてしまうほどでした。

　こうして集まった数多くの作品を並べてみると、カレンダーという媒体のもつ特異性を改めて強く感じずにはいられません。

　第一に、カレンダーは、人が生活していくうえで欠かせない必需品であること。地理上で現在地を確認するように、人は誰しも意識的に、あるいは無意識のうちに時間軸上で現在地を確認しながら生活しています。カレンダーがひとつもない家というのは、そうそう見つからないことでしょう。第二に、長期間の使用を求められること。短くても１か月、万年暦であれば半永久的に使用することになります。第三に、暦＝数字という世界共通の言語によって構成されていること。カレンダーはその制作国がどこであろうと世界中で使用できる、ボーダーレスなツールです。第四として、このように万人向けという性質をもちながらも、カレンダーはある意味で非常にターゲットを絞ったツールであることを挙げたいと思います。私たちが一年をともに過ごす一冊を選ぶとき、そこには何かしらの目的や基準があります。インテリア性を求めるなら部屋のイメージにあったもの、機能性を求めるなら数字が見やすくて、書き込み用の余白があるもの、というように。時にはそれらの意図を忘れ、ひと目ぼれのように選ぶこともありますが…　そうして、企業から届いたり、店頭で目にしたりする多種多様なカレンダーの中から自分に合う一冊を選ぶわけです。

　さて、私たち編集スタッフは日ごろ、様々なグラフィック・ツールを、作り手の想いとそれを受け取る顧客を結ぶという意味でコミュニケーション・ツールと呼んでいますが、この企画を進行して、カレンダーほどその呼称にふさわしいツールはないように思えました。そこで本書は、作り手の制作意図と顧客の要望に着目をして構成しました。掲載作品をプロモーション用とセールス用にカテゴライズすることで、作り手の意図を明確にし、各カテゴリーに多くの作品のタイプを揃えることで、それを選ぶ様々な顧客の姿を反映しようと試みたのです。その結果、次のようなことが見えてきました。

　まず、プロモーション編では、企業の個性とクリエイターの個性が共鳴した、素晴らしい作品が目立ちました。昨今の経済状況も理由のひとつでしょうが、企業プロモーションの一環で制作されるカレンダーは減少傾向にあるといいます。そこをあえて作り続けている企業は、カレンダーという媒体の性質をしっかりと認識しているということなのでしょう。セールス編では、そのバラエティの豊かさに驚かされました。5年前に発行した前作では、掲載作品をタイポグラフィーや写真などのメインとなるヴィジュアル別にカテゴライズしましたが、今回はそのどれにも属さないような個性ある作品が多くありました。多様化した顧客の要望がデザインの可能性をさらに広げたように思えます。更に全体を通して見ると、カレンダーとしての機能にとどまらない付加機能を加えたり、点字対応にしたりとデザインのバリアフリー化の傾向も見て取れました。

　皆さんは本書をご覧になってどのような感想をもたれるのでしょうか。カレンダーを使うときの楽しさに "めくる楽しみ" があります。本書のページをめくる皆さんに、そんな楽しみをご提供できればこのうえない幸せです。

最後に、長期にわたり快くご協力いただきました出品者の皆さま、この場を借りてお礼申し上げます。
ありがとうございました。

ピエ・ブックス　編集部

Foreword

The planning for this book began at the end of the year, when bookstore and variety shop windows were alive with calendars. With the aim of creating "a collection as rich in variation as in quality of design," we set about the long process of collecting works. Day after day unique pieces arrived from creative people near and far. Opening the packages and examining the contents was such a delight, we often forgot it was "work." And with this large array of works spread out before us, we had a renewed sense of how distinctive the medium known as the calendar really is.

Firstly, calendars rank among the necessities of life. Just as we confirm our locations geographically, be it consciously or subconsciously we live our lives confirming our location on the axis of time. It would be a rarity to finds a household today without a single calendar. Secondly, calendars demand long-term use: at their shortest, one month, and perpetual calendars··· virtually forever. Thirdly, calendars are composed of numbers which are a universal language. No matter where a calendar is produced, it is a borderless tool that can be used worldwide. Fourthly, while calendars characteristically can be used by one and all, they are also a tool that can be focused to very specific targets. There are generally some objectives and/or criteria involved in selecting the calendars we plan to live with for the coming year: if it is to form an interior design element, the overall image of the room comes into play; if one is looking for function, readability and sufficient white space for notes become issues. Sometimes people forget purpose all together, and just pick something they love at first sight··· Thus, from all the calendars received from companies or seen in stores, people select the one that suits them.

Our editorial staff uses the term "communication tool" to refer to graphic applications that link the intent of their producers with their recipients; and in the making of this book, we have come to believe that no graphic application suits that term better than calendars do. We composed the book with awareness of both the intent of producers and the demands of their customers. Categorizing the works as promotional or sales pieces made the intent behind the works clear, and by showing a rich assortment of works in each category, we hoped to reflect an image of the various customers that choose them. In the process we observed the following.
The promotion section features fantastic works that resound with the individualism of the companies and designers that produce them. Perhaps due to the recent economic climate, calendars produced as part of company promotions are on the decline. The companies that continue to produce them, however, appear to be well aware of their properties as a medium. The sales section on the other hand shows astounding variety. In our previous calendar collection published five years ago we categorized works by their main visual element-typographic, photographic, etc. This time there were too many unique works that elude such categorization. We see this trend as the diversification of customer demands further expanding the possibilities of design. Looking at the collection overall, we saw added functions that go beyond the those typical of the calendar, and the inclusion of braille type as a reflection of the barrier-free trend in design.

We wonder what impressions our readers will have. Part of the fun of using a calendar is turning the pages. Nothing would please us more than to provide the page-turners of this book that pleasure.

Finally, we would like to take this opportunity to express our gratitude to all those who readily contributed their work. Thank you.

PIE BOOKS

Credit Format

クレジットフォーマット

A　作品タイトル　Work title
　　使用年度　The use year
　　製作国　Production country

B　クライアントの業種　Type of business

C　CL：クライアント　Client
　　CD：クリエイティブ・ディレクター　Creative Director
　　AD：アート・ディレクター　Art Director
　　D：デザイナー　Designer
　　P：フォトグラファー　Photographer
　　I：イラストレーター　Illustrator
　　CW：コピーライター　Copywriter
　　DF：制作会社　Design firm
　　S：作品提供　Submittor

・上記以外の製作者呼称は省略せずに掲載しています。
　Full name of all others involved in the creation / production of the work.

・クレジットは、作品提供者の意向によりデータの一部を記載していない場合があります。
　Please note that some credit date has been omitted at the request of the submittor.

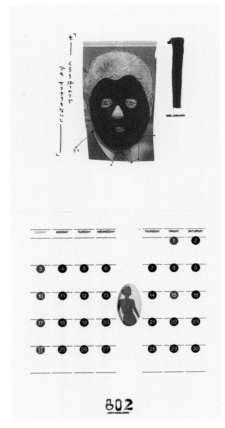

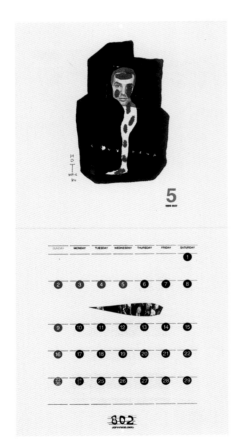

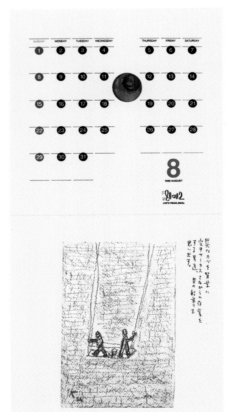

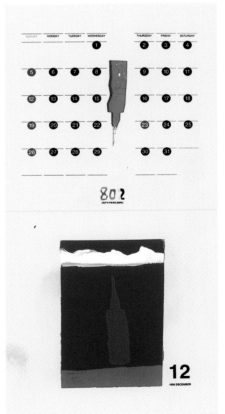

FM802カレンダー　FM802 Calendar　1999　JAPAN

FMラジオ放送局　FM radio station
CL: FM802　AD: 長友啓典　Keisuke Nagatomo　D: 前橋隆道　Takamichi Maebashi　I: 黒田征太郎　Seitaro Kuroda　DF, S: ケイツー　K2

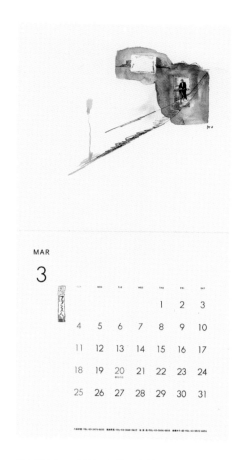

FEB

2

SUN	MON	TUE	WED	THU	FRI	SAT
				1	2	3
4	5	6	7	8	9	10
11	12	13	14	15	16	17
18	19	20	21	22	23	24
25	26	27	28			

MAR

3

SUN	MON	TUE	WED	THU	FRI	SAT
				1	2	3
4	5	6	7	8	9	10
11	12	13	14	15	16	17
18	19	20	21	22	23	24
25	26	27	28	29	30	31

APR

4

SUN	MON	TUE	WED	THU	FRI	SAT
1	2	3	4	5	6	7
8	9	10	11	12	13	14
15	16	17	18	19	20	21
22	23	24	25	26	27	28
29	30					

AUG

8

SUN	MON	TUE	WED	THU	FRI	SAT
			1	2	3	4
5	6	7	8	9	10	11
12	13	14	15	16	17	18
19	20	21	22	23	24	25
26	27	28	29	30	31	

DEC

12

SUN	MON	TUE	WED	THU	FRI	SAT
						1
2	3	4	5	6	7	8
9	10	11	12	13	14	15
16	17	18	19	20	21	22
23	24	25	26	27	28	29
30	31					

焼肉フランス人カレンダー　Yakiniku France-Jin Calendar　2001　JAPAN
飲食店　Restaurant
CL: 焼肉フランス人　Yakiniku France-Jin　AD: 長友啓典　Keisuke Nagatomo　D: 柴田まゆ　Mayu Shibata　I: 黒田征太郎　Seitaro Kuroda　DF, S: ケイツー　K2

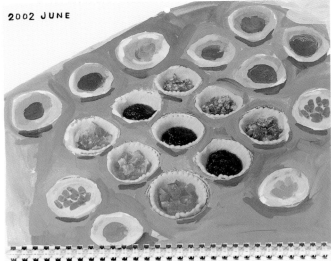

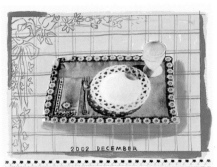

HAKKA CALENDAR 2002　JAPAN

アパレル及び飲食店・雑貨店経営　Apparel, Restaurant & Miscellaneous goods shop
CL: ファッション須賀　FASHION SUGA CO.,LTD.　I: 飯田　淳　Jun Iida　DF: シャワーズ　SHOWERS　S: ファッション須賀　FASHION SUGA CO.,LTD.

MONDAY	TUESDAY	WEDNESDAY	THURSDAY	FRIDAY	SATURDAY	SUNDAY
24	25	26	27	28	1	2
3	4	5	6	7	8	9
10	11	12	13	14	15	16
17	18	19	20	21	22	23
24 31	25	26	27	28	29	30

MARCH　　　　　　　　　　　　　　　2003

MONDAY	TUESDAY	WEDNESDAY	THURSDAY	FRIDAY	SATURDAY	SUNDAY
28	29	30	1	2	3	4
5	6	7	8	9	10	11
12	13	14	15	16	17	18
19	20	21	22	23	24	25
26	27	28	29	30	31	

MAY　　　　　　　　　　　　　　　　2003

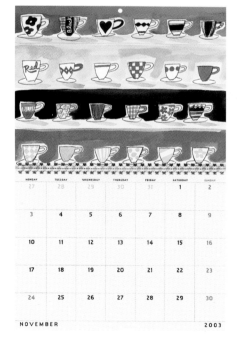

MONDAY	TUESDAY	WEDNESDAY	THURSDAY	FRIDAY	SATURDAY	SUNDAY
30	1	2	3	4	5	6
7	8	9	10	11	12	13
14	15	16	17	18	19	20
21	22	23	24	25	26	27
28	29	30	31	1	2	3

JULY　　　　　　　　　　　　　　　2003

MONDAY	TUESDAY	WEDNESDAY	THURSDAY	FRIDAY	SATURDAY	SUNDAY
27	28	29	30	31	1	2
3	4	5	6	7	8	9
10	11	12	13	14	15	16
17	18	19	20	21	22	23
24	25	26	27	28	29	30

NOVEMBER　　　　　　　　　　　　　2003

HAKKA CALENDAR 2003　JAPAN
アパレル及び飲食店・雑貨店経営　Apparel, Restaurant & Miscellaneous goods shop
CL: ファッション須賀　FASHION SUGA CO.,LTD.　I: 飯田　淳　Jun Iida　DF: シャワーズ　SHOWERS　S: ファッション須賀　FASHION SUGA CO.,LTD.

ふるさとの名山　The Great Mountains in Japan　2001　JAPAN
商社　Trade company
CL: イワタニ産業　Iwatani International Corporation　CD: 伊藤理次　Tadayuki Ito　AD, I, S: 木田安彦　Yasuhiko kida　AD, D: 呂　錦源　Kenny ROI Kingen　DF: ケニーデザイン室　Kenny Design office

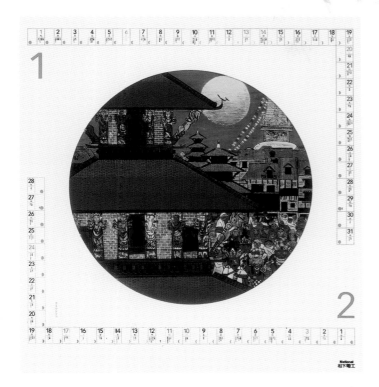

世界遺産 The World Heritage　2002　JAPAN
電気・建材メーカー Electric manufacturer
CL: 松下電工 Matsushita Electric Works,Ltd.　CD, AD, D, I, S: 木田安彦 Yasuhiko Kida　D: 新里一裕 Kazuhiro Shinzato　CW: 横山俊夫 Toshio Yokoyama　DF: アラタデザインオフィス Arata Design office

一
JANUARY

日	月	火	水	木	金	土
30	31	1	2	3	4	5
6	7	8	9	10	11	12
13	14	15	16	17	18	19
20	21	22	23	24	25	26
27	28	29	30	31	1	2
3	4	5	6	7	8	9

モリサワ

五
MAY

日	月	火	水	木	金	土
28	29	30	1	2	3	4
5	6	7	8	9	10	11
12	13	14	15	16	17	18
19	20	21	22	23	24	25
26	27	28	29	30	31	1
2	3	4	5	6	7	8

モリサワ

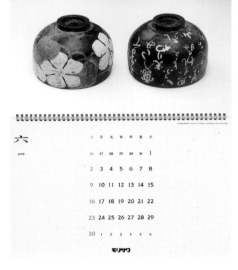

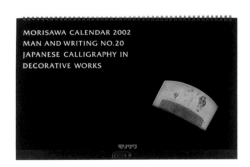

MORISAWA CALENDAR 2002
MAN AND WRITING NO.20
JAPANESE CALLIGRAPHY IN
DECORATIVE WORKS

モリサワ

六
JUNE

日	月	火	水	木	金	土
26	27	28	29	30	31	1
2	3	4	5	6	7	8
9	10	11	12	13	14	15
16	17	18	19	20	21	22
23	24	25	26	27	28	29
30	1	2	3	4	5	6

モリサワ

九
SEPTEMBER

日	月	火	水	木	金	土
1	2	3	4	5	6	7
8	9	10	11	12	13	14
15	16	17	18	19	20	21
22	23	24	25	26	27	28
29	1	2	3	4	5	
6	7	8	9	10	11	12

モリサワ

MORISAWA CALENDAR 2002 MAN AND WRITING NO.20 "JAPANESE CALLIGRAPHY IN DECORATIVE WORKS"　JAPAN
フォント・印刷関連　Font & Printing equipment
CL: モリサワ　MORISAWA & COMPANY LTD.　AD, D: 田中一光　Ikko Tanaka　D: 大内　修　Osamu Ouchi　Editor: 加藤國康　Kuniyasu Kato　Writer: 西岡康宏　Yasuhiro Nishioka　P: 畠山　崇　Takashi Hatakeyama
Pri: 大日本印刷　Dai Nippon Printing Co.,Ltd.　S: モリサワ　MORISAWA & COMPANY LTD.

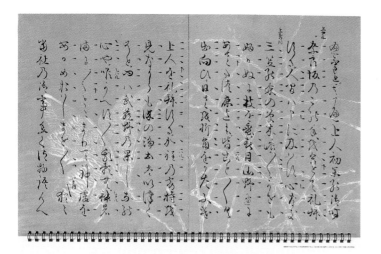

弥生
3
MAR. 2003

日	月	火	水	木	金	土
						1
2	3	4	5	6	7	8
9	10	11	12	13	14	15
16	17	18	19	20	21	22
23	24	25	26	27	28	29
30	31					

皐月
5
MAY 2003

日	月	火	水	木	金	土
				1	2	3
4	5	6	7	8	9	10
11	12	13	14	15	16	17
18	19	20	21	22	23	24
25	26	27	28	29	30	31

睦月
1
JAN. 2003

日	月	火	水	木	金	土
			1	2	3	4
5	6	7	8	9	10	11
12	13	14	15	16	17	18
19	20	21	22	23	24	25
26	27	28	29	30	31	

霜月
11
NOV. 2003

日	月	火	水	木	金	土
						1
2	3	4	5	6	7	8
9	10	11	12	13	14	15
16	17	18	19	20	21	22
23	24	25	26	27	28	29
30						

MORISAWA CALENDAR 2003 MAN AND WRITING NO.21　"Japanese Calligraphy in Narrative Literature"　　JAPAN
フォント・印刷関連　Font & Printing equipment
CL: モリサワ　MORISAWA & COMPANY LTD.　Planner: 田中一光　Ikko Tanaka　Supervisor: 樺山紘一　Kouichi Kabayama　AD, D: 木下勝弘　Katsuhiro Kinoshita　Editor: 加藤國康　Kuniyasu Kato
P: 畠山　崇　Takashi Hatakeyama　Pri: 凸版印刷　Toppan Printing Co.,Ltd.　S: モリサワ　MORISAWA & COMPANY LTD.

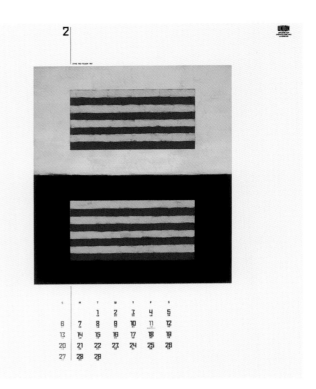

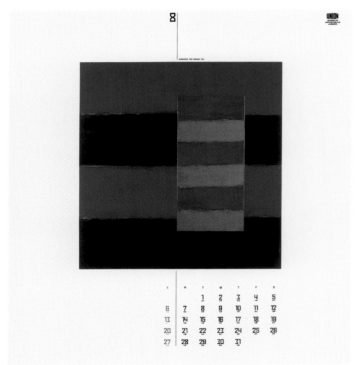

SEAN SCULLY　2000　JAPAN

建設環境金属製品の製造・販売　Manufacture & Sales of various architectual amenities & components
CL: ユニオン　UNION CO.,LTD.　AD, D: 松井桂三　Keizo Matsui　Artist: SEAN SCULLY　DF, S: ハンドレッド デザインインク　HUNDRED DESIGN INC.

GIO PONTI　2003　JAPAN
建設環境金属製品の製造・販売　Manufacture & Sales of various architectual amenities & components
CL: ユニオン　UNION CO.,LTD.　AD, D: 松井桂三　Keizo Matsui　D: 中村　愛　Ai Nakamura　Artist: GIO PONTI　DF, S: ハンドレッド デザインインク　HUNDRED DESIGN INC.

住宅産業　Housing industry

美 し い く ら し
デイヴィッド・ホックニー作品集

1		mon	tue	wed	thu	fri	sat		mon	tue	wed	thu	fri	sat	2
JANUARY	1		2	3	4	5	6					1	2	3	FEBRUARY
			9	10	11	12	13		5	6	7	8	9	10	
			15	16	17	18	19	20		13	14	15	16	17	
			22	23	24	25	26	27		19	20	21	22	23	24
	28		29	30	31					26	27	28			

2 0 0 1　P A N A H O M E　C A L E N D A R

「美しいくらし」デヴィッド・ホックニー作品集　Beatiful Life:David Hockney　2001　JAPAN
住宅産業　Housing industry
CL: ナショナル住宅産業　PANAHOME Co.,Ltd.　CD: 大日本印刷メディアクリエイト関西　Dainippon Printing Co.,Ltd.　AD, D: 勝井三雄　Mitsuo Katsui　D: 石橋昌子　Masako Ishibashi
Artist: David Hockney　DF, S: 勝井デザイン事務所　Katsui Design Office

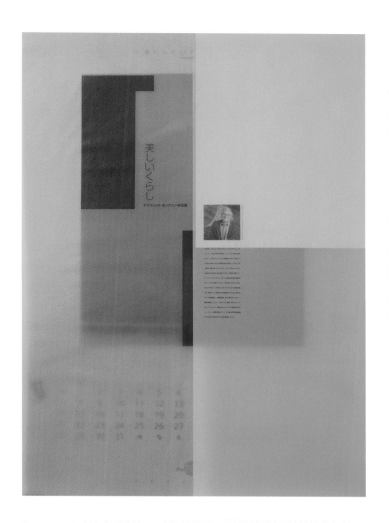

Calendar 2003 Phollage by Shin Matsunaga　　JAPAN
建材事業　Building material business
CL: YKK AP Inc.　　CD, AD, D, P: 松永　真　Shin Matsunaga　D: 伊藤英典　Hidenori Ito　S: 松永真デザイン事務所　Shin Matsunaga Design Inc.

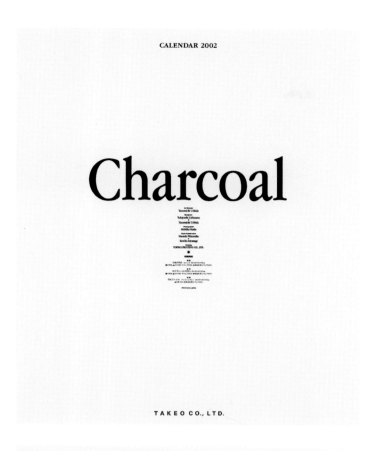

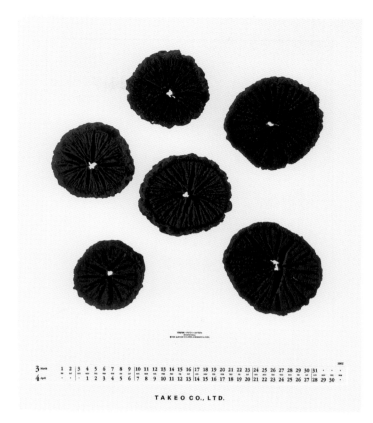

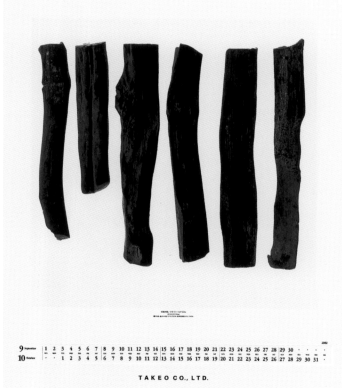

Charcoal　2002　JAPAN
商業　Commerce
CL: 竹尾　TAKEO CO.,LTD.　CD, AD: 内田靖通　Yasumichi Uchida　D: 牛山幸吉　Yukiyoshi Ushiyama　P: 工藤哲彦　Akihiko Kudo　S: 凸版印刷　TOPPAN PRINTING CO.,LTD.

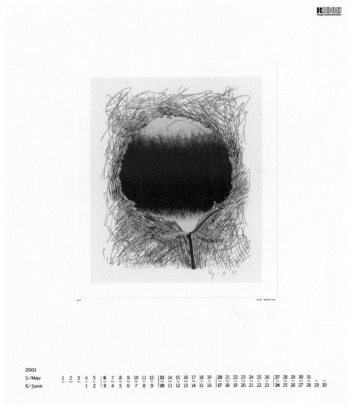

Rainbow Rainbow 虹　2001　JAPAN

精密機械　Precision instruments
CL: リコー　RICOH CO.,LTD.　Planner: 髙山峰治　Mineharu Takayama　CD, AD, D: 内田靖通　Yasumichi Uchida　D: 山本　寿　Toshi Yamamoto : 町田和彦　Kazuhiko Machida　Artist: 饗噱　AY-O
S: 凸版印刷　TOPPAN PRINTING CO.,LTD.

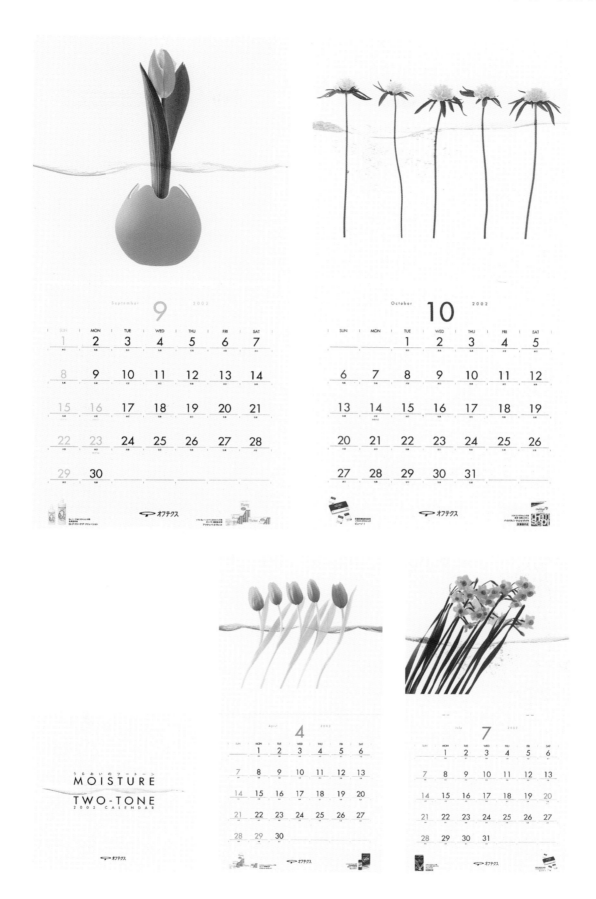

MOISTURE TWO TONE　2002　JAPAN

薬品メーカー　Medicine manufacturer

CL: オフテクス　OPHTECS　　AD: 高橋善丸　Yoshimaru Takahashi　　D: 菊沢良仁　Yoshihito Kikuzawa　　DF, S: 広告丸　kokokumaru inc.

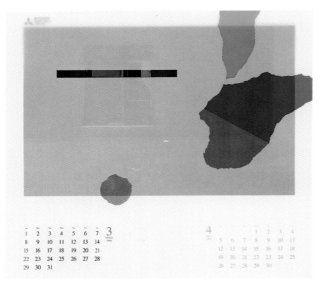

1998

M E D I T E R R A N E A N

C O L O R

三菱 トレーシングペーパーカレンダー　**MITSUBISHI TRANSPARENT PAPER CALENDAR**　1998　JAPAN

製紙　Paper manufacturer
CL: 三菱製紙　MITSUBISHI PAPER MILLS LIMITED　AD: 小島良平　Ryohei Kojima　D: 北島　栄　Sakae Kitajima　P: Jeffrey Becom : 坂本　勉　Tsutomu Sakamoto
DF, S: 小島良平デザイン事務所　RYOHEI KOJIMA DESIGN OFFICE

Sun	Mon	Tue	Wed	Thu	Fri	Sat	
		1	2	3	4	5	**9** September 1998
6	7	8	9	10	11	12	
13	14	15	16	17	18	19	
20	21	22	23	24	25	26	
27	28	29	30				

10 October 1998	Sun	Mon	Tue	Wed	Thu	Fri	Sat
					1	2	3
	4	5	6	7	8	9	10
	11	12	13	14	15	16	17
	18	19	20	21	22	23	24
	25	26	27	28	29	30	31

10 October 1998	Sun	Mon	Tue	Wed	Thu	Fri	Sat
					1	2	3
	4	5	6	7	8	9	10
	11	12	13	14	15	16	17
	18	19	20	21	22	23	24
	25	26	27	28	29	30	31

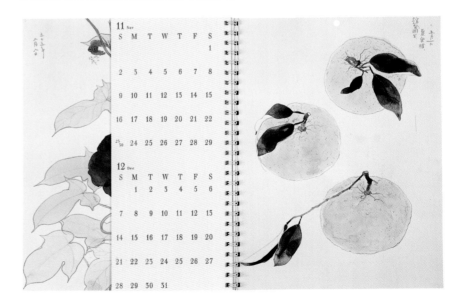

Art Calendar 2003 Konno Chuichi-Tranquil-　JAPAN
美術商　Fine art quotient
CL: トゥレス　Torres Inc.　CD: 今野怜子　Reiko Konno　AD: 原　耕一　Koichi Hara　D: 渡邊隆雄　Takao Watanabe　Artist: 今野忠一　Chuichi Konno　DF, S: トラウト　Trout Inc.

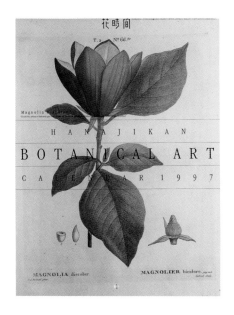

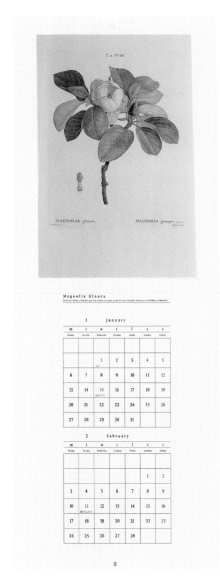

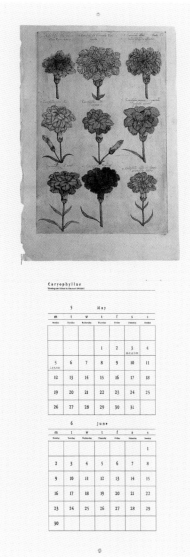

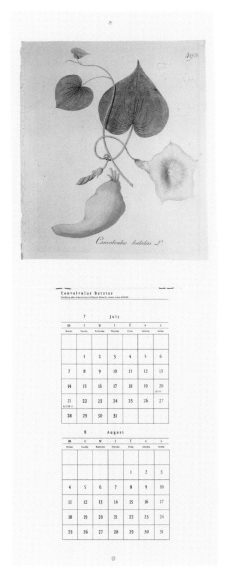

Supplement to "HANAJIKAN" BOTANICAL ART CALENDAR 1997 「花時間」付録 ボタニカルアートカレンダー1997年　JAPAN

出版　Publisher
CL: 角川書店　KADOKAWA SHOTEN PUBLISHING CO., LTD.　AD: 岡本一宣　Issen Okamoto　D: 小埜田尚子　Naoko Onoda　P: 青木健二　Kenji Aoki　Photography cooperation: アリア　Aria
DF, S: 岡本一宣デザイン事務所　Okamoto Issen Graphic Design Company Ltd.

November　December

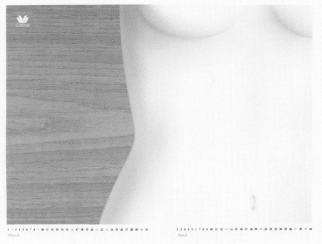

2003 ワコール カレンダー　2003 WACOAL CALENDAR　JAPAN
女性洋装下着の製造・卸・販売 Manufacture of the woman Western-style clothes underwear
CL: ワコール　WACOAL CORP.　CD: 大八木雅夫　Masao Oyagi　AD, D: 前川詩乃　Shino Maekawa　CG Engineer: 山下直人／クォーレ　Naoto Yamashita / CUORE
DF: ワコール宣伝部　WACOAL CORP.ADVERTISING DIV.　S: ワコール　WACOAL CORP.

1999 ワコール カレンダー　1999 WACOAL CALENDAR　JAPAN

女性洋装下着の製造・卸・販売　Manufacture of the woman Western-style clothes underwear

CL: ワコール　WACOAL CORP.　CD, AD: 佐々木豊　Yutaka Sasaki　D: 下田理恵　Rie Shimoda：村上千博　Chihiro Murakami　I: 今井正博　Masahiro Imai　DF: 日本デザインセンター　NIPPON DESIGN CENTER
S: ワコール　WACOAL CORP.

 January / February　1 MON 2 TUE 3 WED 4 THU 5 FRI 6 SAT 7 SUN 8 MON 9 TUE 10 WED 11 THU 12 FRI 13 SAT 14 SUN 15 MON 16 TUE 17 WED 18 THU 19 FRI 20 SAT 21 SUN 22 MON 23 TUE 24 WED 25 THU 26 FRI 27 SAT 28 SUN 29 MON 30 TUE 31 WED
1 2 3 4 5 6 7 8 9 10 11 12 13 14 15 16 17 18 19 20 21 22 23 24 25 26 27 28

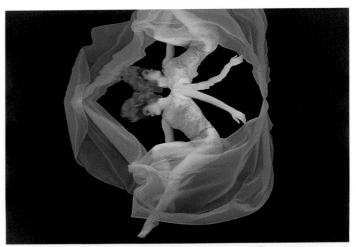

March / April

September / October

2001 ワコール カレンダー　2001 WACOAL CALENDAR　JAPAN

女性洋装下着の製造・卸・販売　Manufacture of the woman Western-style clothes underwear
CL: ワコール　WACOAL CORP.　CD: 大八木雅夫　Masao Oyagi　AD: 今西清美　Kiyomi Imanishi : 藤脇慎吾　Shingo Fujiwaki　D: 手島貴乃　Takano Teshima　P: Haward Schatz　CW: 渡邊聡子　Satoko Watanabe
DF: ワコール宣伝部＋藤脇デザイン　WACOAL CORP.ADVERTISING DIV.＋FUJIWAKI DESIGN OFFICE　S: ワコール　WACOAL CORP.

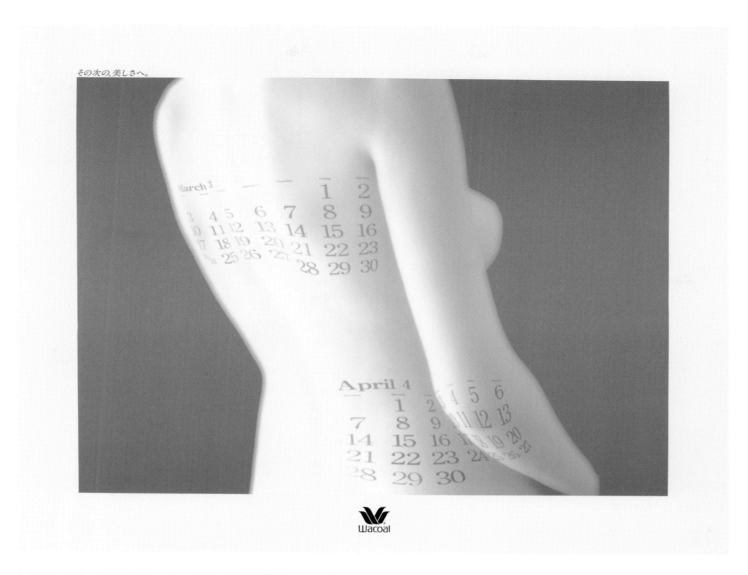

2002 ワコール カレンダー 2002 WACOAL CALENDAR   JAPAN
女性洋装下着の製造・卸・販売 Manufacture of the woman Western-style clothes underwear
CL: ワコール WACOAL CORP.   CD, AD: 尾崎建一 Kenichi Ozaki   D: 永嶋憲次 Kenji Nagashima : 内田百合香 Yurika Uchida   P: 今川　真 Makoto Imagawa   CG Engineer: 三谷　正 Tadashi Mitani
DF: ワコール宣伝部 WACOAL CORP.ADVERTISING DIV.   S: ワコール WACOAL CORP.

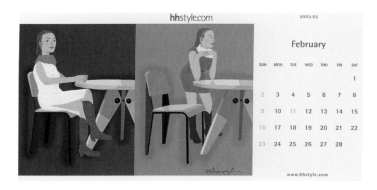

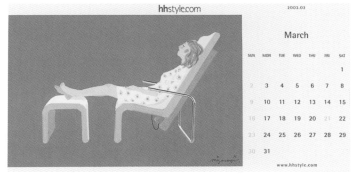

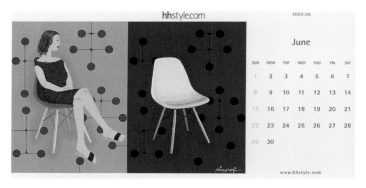

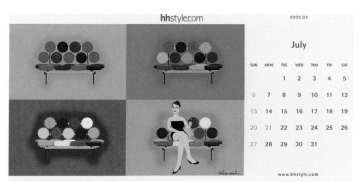

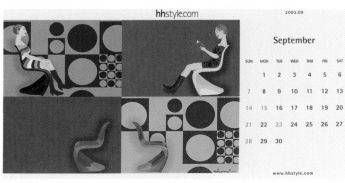

hhstyle.com calendar　2003　JAPAN
家具・インテリア雑貨の販売　Furniture supplier
CL: エイチエイチスタイルドットコム　hhstyle.com　AD, D, I: 溝呂木　陽　Akira Mizorogi　S: エイチエイチスタイルドットコム　hhstyle.com

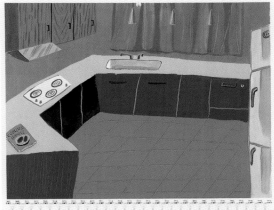

MONDAY	TUESDAY	WEDNESDAY	THURSDAY	FRIDAY	SATURDAY	SUNDAY
1	2	3	4	5	6	7
8	9	10	11	12	13	14
15	16	17	18	19	20	21
22	23	24	25	26	27	28
29	30	31				

JANUARY **2001**

MONDAY	TUESDAY	WEDNESDAY	THURSDAY	FRIDAY	SATURDAY	SUNDAY
						1
2	3	4	5	6	7	8
9	10	11	12	13	14	15
16	17	18	19	20	21	22
23	24	25	26	27	28	29
30						

APRIL **2001**

MONDAY	TUESDAY	WEDNESDAY	THURSDAY	FRIDAY	SATURDAY	SUNDAY
				1	2	3
4	5	6	7	8	9	10
11	12	13	14	15	16	17
18	19	20	21	22	23	24
25	26	27	28	29	30	

JUNE **2001**

MONDAY	TUESDAY	WEDNESDAY	THURSDAY	FRIDAY	SATURDAY	SUNDAY
					1	2
3	4	5	6	7	8	9
10	11	12	13	14	15	16
17	18	19	20	21	22	23
24	25	26	27	28	29	30
31						

DECEMBER **2001**

HAKKA CALENDAR 2001　JAPAN
アパレル及び飲食店・雑貨店経営　Apparel, Restaurant & Miscellaneous goods shop
CL: ファッション須賀　FASHION SUGA CO.,LTD.　I: 飯田　淳　Jun Iida　DF: シャワーズ　SHOWERS　S: ファッション須賀　FASHION SUGA CO.,LTD.

オーパ カレンダー　Opa Calendar　2002　JAPAN

自動車の製造・販売　Motor manufacturer & dealer
CL: トヨタ自動車　TOYOTA MOTOR CORPORATION　AD: 浜島達也　Tatsuya Hamajima　AD, D: 寒河江亘太　Kouta Sagae　I: 田辺ヒロシ　Hiroshi Tanabe
S: 電通　Dentsu inc. : シューデザイン　Chou Design Co.,Ltd.

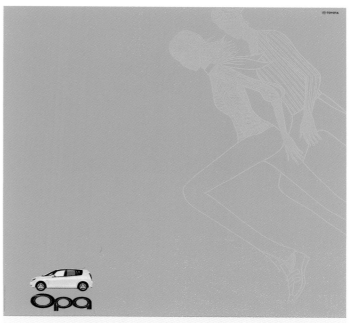

SUNDAY	MONDAY	TUESDAY	WEDNESDAY	THURSDAY	FRIDAY	SATURDAY
				1	2	3
4	5	6	7	8	9	10
11	12	13	14	15	16	17
18	19	20	21	22	23	24
25	26	27	28	29	30	31

J A N U A R Y　　　　　　　　　　1 9 9 8

SUNDAY	MONDAY	TUESDAY	WEDNESDAY	THURSDAY	FRIDAY	SATURDAY
	1	2	3	4	5	6
7	8	9	10	11	12	13
14	15	16	17	18	19	20
21	22	23	24	25	26	27
28	29	30				

J U N E　　　　　　　　　　1 9 9 8

SUNDAY	MONDAY	TUESDAY	WEDNESDAY	THURSDAY	FRIDAY	SATURDAY
			1	2	3	4
5	6	7	8	9	10	11
12	13	14	15	16	17	18
19	20	21	22	23	24	25
26	27	28	29	30	31	

J U L Y　　　　　　　　　　1 9 9 8

SUNDAY	MONDAY	TUESDAY	WEDNESDAY	THURSDAY	FRIDAY	SATURDAY
				1	2	3
4	5	6	7	8	9	10
11	12	13	14	15	16	17
18	19	20	21	22	23	24
25	26	27	28	29	30	31

O C T O B E R　　　　　　　　　　1 9 9 8

HAKKA CALENDAR 1998　JAPAN

アパレル及び飲食店・雑貨店経営　Apparel, Restaurant & Miscellaneous goods shop
CL: ファッション須賀　FASHION SUGA CO.,LTD.　I: 飯田　淳　Jun Iida　DF: シャワーズ　SHOWERS　S: ファッション須賀　FASHION SUGA CO.,LTD.

Spick and Span CALENDAR CATALOGUE　2002　JAPAN

アパレル　Apparel
CL: ベイクルーズ　BAYCREW'S co.,ltd.　CD, AD, D, I, DF, S: ベイクルーズ クリエイティブサービスデザイン　BAYCREW'S co.,ltd. / creative service design

Dominique Corbasson 2002 Calendar　JAPAN

アパレル　Apparel
CL: ジュン　JUN Co.,Ltd.　CD, AD, D, DF: クロスワールドコネクションズ　Cross World Connections　I: Dominique Corbasson　S: ジュン　JUN Co.,Ltd.

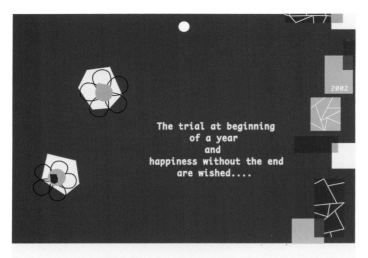

The trial at beginning
of a year
and
happiness without the end
are wished....

2002

a substantial life

2002

		JANUALY							FEBRUARY				
Sun	Mon	Tue	Wed	Thu	Fri	Sat	Sun	Mon	Tue	Wed	Thu	Fri	Sat
		1	2	3	4	5						1	2
6	7	8	9	10	11	12	3	4	5	6	7	8	9
13	14	15	16	17	18	19	10	11	12	13	14	15	16
20	21	22	23	24	25	26	17	18	19	20	21	22	23
27	28	29	30	31			24	25	26	27	28		

SM2
Té chichi

		SEPTEMBER							OCTOBER				
Sun	Mon	Tue	Wed	Thu	Fri	Sat	Sun	Mon	Tue	Wed	Thu	Fri	Sat
1	2	3	4	5	6	7			1	2	3	4	5
8	9	10	11	12	13	14	6	7	8	9	10	11	12
15	16	17	18	19	20	21	13	14	15	16	17	18	19
22	23	24	25	26	27	28	20	21	22	23	24	25	26
29	30						27	28	29	30	31		

SM2
Té chichi

2002
calender
SM2
and
Tèchichi

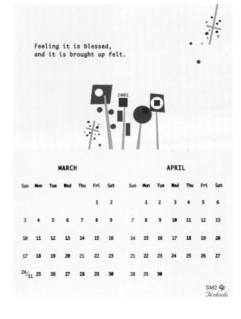

Feeling it is blessed,
and it is brought up felt.

2002

・・・ rainy rainy DAYS

2002

		MARCH							APRIL				
Sun	Mon	Tue	Wed	Thu	Fri	Sat	Sun	Mon	Tue	Wed	Thu	Fri	Sat
					1	2		1	2	3	4	5	6
3	4	5	6	7	8	9	7	8	9	10	11	12	13
10	11	12	13	14	15	16	14	15	16	17	18	19	20
17	18	19	20	21	22	23	21	22	23	24	25	26	27
24/31	25	26	27	28	29	30	28	29	30				

		MAY							JUNE				
Sun	Mon	Tue	Wed	Thu	Fri	Sat	Sun	Mon	Tue	Wed	Thu	Fri	Sat
		1	2	3	4								1
5	6	7	8	9	10	11	2	3	4	5	6	7	8
12	13	14	15	16	17	18	9	10	11	12	13	14	15
19	20	21	22	23	24	25	16	17	18	19	20	21	22
26	27	28	29	30	31		23/30	24	25	26	27	28	29

SM2
Té chichi

SM2 2002 calendar　JAPAN

洋服・雑貨の企画・製造・販売　Planning, Manufacture, Sales of clothes & miscellaneous goods
CL: キャン　CAN Co.,Ltd.　CD, S: キャン　CAN Co.,Ltd.

JANUARY
wed thu fri sat sun mon tue wed thu fri sat sun mon tue wed thu fri sat sun mon tue wed thu fri
1 2 3 4 5 6 7 8 9 10 11 12 13 14 15 16 17 18 19 20 21 22 23 24 25 26 27 28 29 30 31

FEBRUARY
sat sun mon tue wed thu fri sat sun mon tue wed thu fri sat sun mon tue wed thu fri sat sun mon tue wed thu fri
1 2 3 4 5 6 7 8 9 10 11 12 13 14 15 16 17 18 19 20 21 22 23 24 25 26 27 28

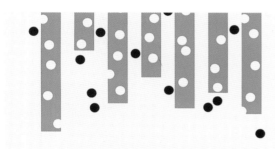

MAY
thu fri sat sun mon tue wed thu fri sat sun mon tue wed thu fri sat sun mon tue wed thu fri sat
1 2 3 4 5 6 7 8 9 10 11 12 13 14 15 16 17 18 19 20 21 22 23 24 25 26 27 28 29 30 31

JUNE
sun mon tue wed thu fri sat sun mon tue wed thu fri sat sun mon tue wed thu fri sat sun mon
1 2 3 4 5 6 7 8 9 10 11 12 13 14 15 16 17 18 19 20 21 22 23 24 25 26 27 28 29 30

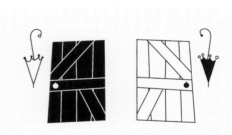

MAY
thu fri sat sun mon tue wed thu fri sat sun mon tue wed thu fri sat sun mon tue wed thu fri sat
1 2 3 4 5 6 7 8 9 10 11 12 13 14 15 16 17 18 19 20 21 22 23 24 25 26 27 28 29 30 31

JUNE
sun mon tue wed thu fri sat sun mon tue wed thu fri sat sun mon tue wed thu fri sat sun mon
1 2 3 4 5 6 7 8 9 10 11 12 13 14 15 16 17 18 19 20 21 22 23 24 25 26 27 28 29 30

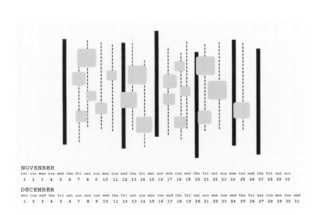

NOVENBER
sat sun mon tue wed thu fri sat sun mon tue wed thu fri sat sun mon tue wed thu fri sat sun mon tue wed thu fri sat sun
1 2 3 4 5 6 7 8 9 10 11 12 13 14 15 16 17 18 19 20 21 22 23 24 25 26 27 28 29 30

DECEMBER
mon tue wed thu fri sat sun mon tue wed thu fri sat sun mon tue wed thu fri sat sun mon tue wed thu fri sat sun mon tue wed
1 2 3 4 5 6 7 8 9 10 11 12 13 14 15 16 17 18 19 20 21 22 23 24 25 26 27 28 29 30 31

NOVENBER
sat sun mon tue wed thu fri sat sun mon tue wed thu fri sat sun mon tue wed thu fri sat sun mon
1 2 3 4 5 6 7 8 9 10 11 12 13 14 15 16 17 18 19 20 21 22 23 24 25 26 27 28 29 30

DECEMBER
mon tue wed thu fri sat sun mon tue wed thu fri sat sun mon tue wed thu fri sat sun mon tue wed thu fri sat sun mon tue wed
1 2 3 4 5 6 7 8 9 10 11 12 13 14 15 16 17 18 19 20 21 22 23 24 25 26 27 28 29 30 31

SM2 2003 calendar　JAPAN

洋服・雑貨の企画・製造・販売　Planning, Manufacture, Sales of clothes & miscellaneous goods
CL: キャン　CAN Co.,Ltd.　CD, S: キャン　CAN Co.,Ltd.

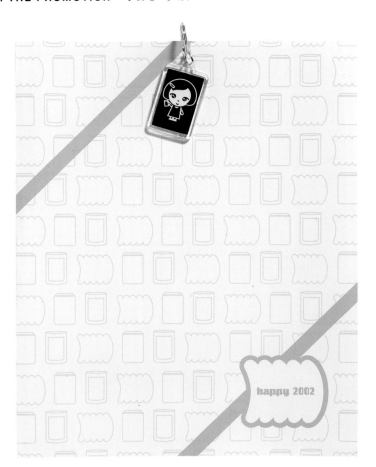

happy 2002

january

O-Shogatsu
On New Year's Day children receive otoshidama, which is money packaged in envelopes as gifts from parents and relatives.

sun	mon	tue	wed	thu	fri	sat
		1 O-Shogatsu	2	3	4	5
6	7	8	9	10	11	12
13	14	15	16	17	18	19
20	21	22	23	24	25	26
27	28	29	30	31		

august

etiquette
Gifts are always wrapped in paper. They are presented and received with a sense of humility and respect. Both hands are used to give the gift with a bow.

sun	mon	tue	wed	thu	fri	sat
				1	2	3
4	5	6	7	8	9	10
11	12	13	14	15	16	17
18	19	20	21	22	23	24
25	26	27	28	29	30	31

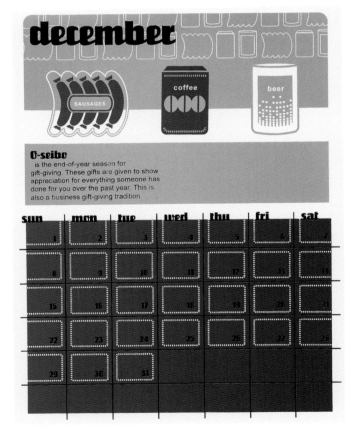

december

O-seibo
is the end-of-year season for gift-giving. These gifts are given to show appreciation for everything someone has done for you over the past year. This is also a business gift-giving tradition.

sun	mon	tue	wed	thu	fri	sat
1	2	3	4	5	6	7
8	9	10	11	12	13	14
15	16	17	18	19	20	21
22	23	24	25	26	27	28
29	30	31				

HAPPY 2002   CANADA
デザイン事務所 Design firm
CL: ESM-ARTIFICIAL   CD, AD, D, I: Mary-Lou Hewlett   AD: Kenn Sakurai   S: ESM-ARTIFICIAL

2000 3 MARCH

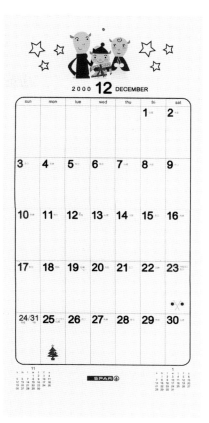

2000 8 AUGUST

2000 12 DECEMBER

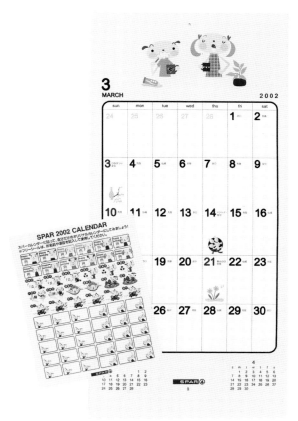

3 MARCH 2002

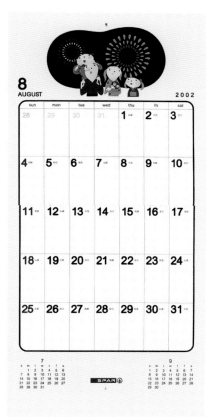

8 AUGUST 2002

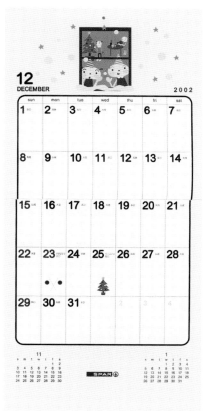

12 DECEMBER 2002

SPAR 2002 CALENDAR

SPAR CALENDAR 2002, 2000 JAPAN

コンビニエンスストア Convenience store
CL: 北海道スパー Hokkaido SPAR　AD, D: 工藤良平 Ryohei Kudo　I: 北原いずみ Izumi Kitahara　DF: ホーム HOME INC.　S: スイスイ Sui Sui,Ltd.

化学製品、食品などの製造・販売 Manufacture, Sales of chemicals & food
CL: 鐘淵化学工業　KANEKA CORPORATION　CD, AD, D, I: 松永　真　Shin Matsunaga　D: 松永真次郎　Shinjiro Matsunaga　S: 松永真デザイン事務所　Shin Matsunaga Design Inc.

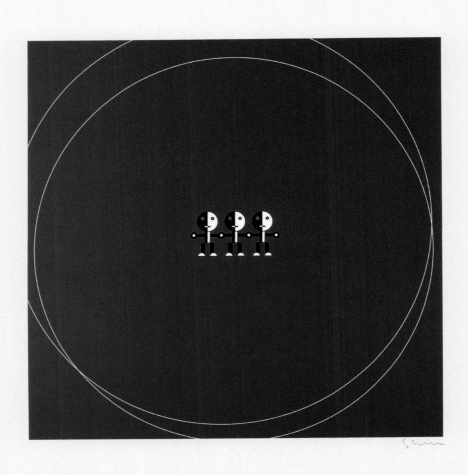

1	SUN	MON	TUE	WED	THU	FRI	SAT		2	SUN	MON	TUE	WED	THU	FRI	SAT
JANUARY	30	31	1	2	3	4	5		FEBRUARY	27	28	29	30	31	1	2
	6	7	8	9	10	11	12			3	4	5	6	7	8	9
	13	14	15	16	17	18	19			10	11	12	13	14	15	16
	20	21	22	23	24	25	26			17	18	19	20	21	22	23
	27	28	29	30	31	1	2			24	25	26	27	28	1	2

Kaneka
鐘淵化学
KANEKA CORPORATION

2002 KANEKA CORPORATION CALENDAR　JAPAN

化学製品、食品などの製造・販売 Manufacture, Sales of chemicals & food
CL: 鐘淵化学工業　KANEKA CORPORATION　CD, AD, D, I: 松永　真　Shin Matsunaga　D: 松永真次郎　Shinjiro Matsunaga　S: 松永真デザイン事務所　Shin Matsunaga Design Inc.

2002

KANEKA

CORPORATION

CALENDAR

Design by Shin Matsunaga

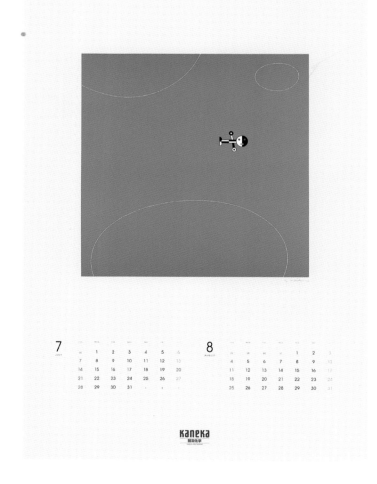

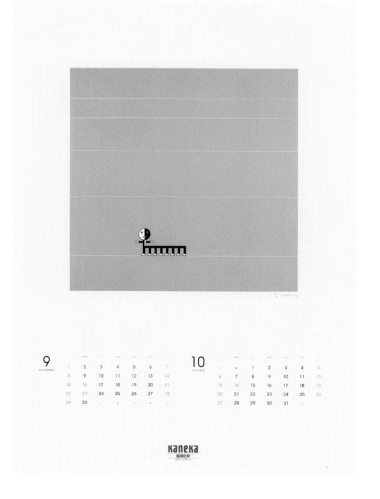

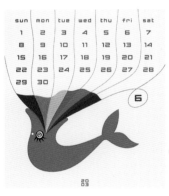

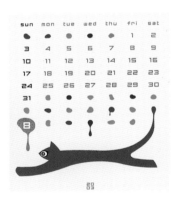

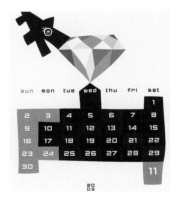

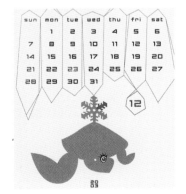

THE 2003 ZOO calendar　JAPAN

デザイン事務所　Design firm
CL: デザイン エンド ラン　design and run　AD, D, I: 大山　武　Takeshi Oyama　DF, S: デザイン エンド ラン　design and run

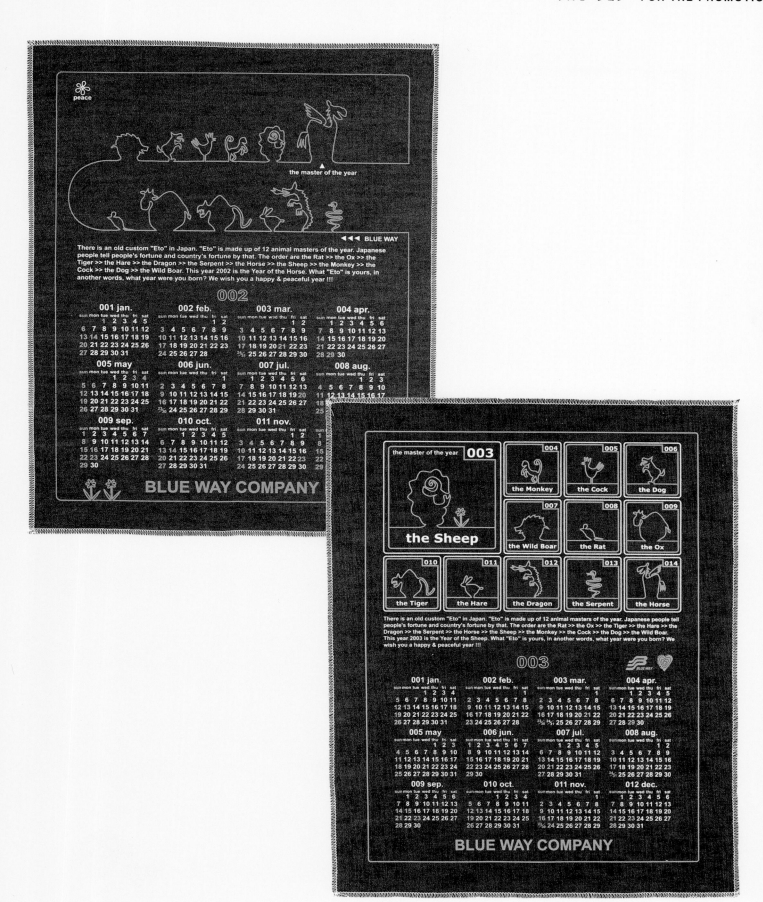

eto   2003, 2002 JAPAN
アパレル Apparel
CL: ブルーウェイ BLUE WAY COMPANY   I: 大島秀一 Shuichi Oshima   S: ブルーウェイ BLUE WAY COMPANY

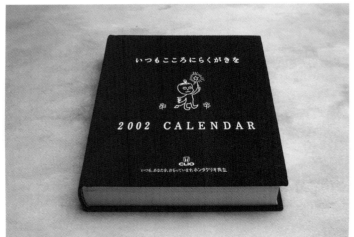

ホンダクリオ共立 2002カレンダー "いつもこころにらくがきを"　Honda Clio Kyoritsu 2002 CALENDAR "Doodling for the Soul"　JAPAN

自動車の販売　Motor dealer

CL: ホンダクリオ共立　Honda Clio Kyoritsu　　CD, CW: こしみず幸三　Kozo Koshimizu　　AD: 清水節江　Setsue Shimizu　　D: 早津悦江　Yoshie Hayatsu　　P: 田中　茂　Shigeru Tanaka　　I: sino

Producer: 関　栄勝　Eikatsu Seki　DF, S: C' Co.,Ltd.

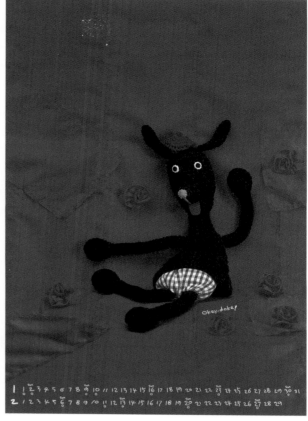

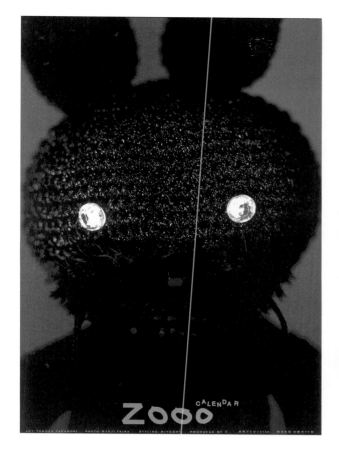

公募ガイド社 2000 カレンダー　Koubo-Guide 2000 CALENDAR　JAPAN

出版 Publisher
CL: 公募ガイド社 Koubo-Guide　CD, CW: こしみず幸三 Kozo Koshimizu　AD: 清水節江 Setsue Shimizu　D: 中村直美 Naomi Nakamura　P: 平　竜二 Ryuji Taira
Artist: 髙森共子 Tomoko Takamori　Stylist: MIYOSHI　DF, S: C' Co.,Ltd.

呉服・宝石等の販売

1
JANUARY

SUN	MON	TUE	WED	THU	FRI	SAT
			1	2	3	4
5	6	7	8	9	10	11
12	13	14	15	16	17	18
19	20	21	22	23	24	25
26	27	28	29	30	31	

3
MARCH

SUN	MON	TUE	WED	THU	FRI	SAT
						1
2	3	4	5	6	7	8
9	10	11	12	13	14	15
16	17	18	19	20	21	22
23/30	24/31	25	26	27	28	29

5
MAY

SUN	MON	TUE	WED	THU	FRI	SAT
				1	2	3
4	5	6	7	8	9	10
11	12	13	14	15	16	17
18	19	20	21	22	23	24
25	26	27	28	29	30	31

7
JULY

SUN	MON	TUE	WED	THU	FRI	SAT
		1	2	3	4	5
6	7	8	9	10	11	12
13	14	15	16	17	18	19
20	21	22	23	24	25	26
27	28	29	30	31		

11
NOVEMBER

SUN	MON	TUE	WED	THU	FRI	SAT
						1
2	3	4	5	6	7	8
9	10	11	12	13	14	15
16	17	18	19	20	21	22
23/30	24	25	26	27	28	29

12
DECEMBER

SUN	MON	TUE	WED	THU	FRI	SAT
	1	2	3	4	5	6
7	8	9	10	11	12	13
14	15	16	17	18	19	20
21	22	23	24	25	26	27
28	29	30	31			

さが美 2003 カレンダー　SAGAMI 2003 CALENDAR　　JAPAN
呉服・宝石等の販売　Sales of fabric for kimono, jewel
CL: さが美　SAGAMI　　CD, AD: 岡島己幸　Miyuki Okajima　　D: 岩野滋子　Shigeko Iwano　　P: 山形秀一　Shuichi Yamagata　　DF, S: エイム　aim

Organic Calendar　オーガニックカレンダー　1999 JAPAN
デザイン事務所　Design firm
CL: デザインユニット リ・ビーンズ　Design Unit Re Beans　AD: 岡　記生　Norio Oka　D, I: 岡　公美　Kumi Oka　S: デザインユニット リ・ビーンズ　Design Unit Re Beans

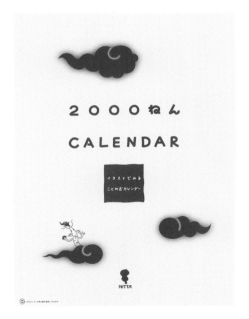

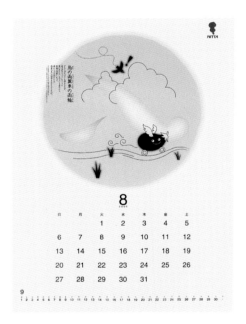

イラストでみることわざカレンダー　Calendar with Illustrations and Proverbs　2000　JAPAN

ゴム・ベルトメーカー　Rubber & Belting manufacturer
CL: ニッタ　NITTA CORPORATION　CD, D: 嶋　高宏　Takahiro Shima　D: 砂田祥江　Sachie Sunada　CW: 山田玲子　Reiko Yamada　DF, S: 嶋デザイン事務所　Shima Design Office

山羊さんゆうびん
作詞者　まど・みちお　　作曲者　團 伊玖磨

白やぎさんから　お手紙　ついた
黒やぎさんたら　読まずに　食べた
しかたが　ないので　お手紙　かいた
さっきの　手紙の　ご用事　なぁに

黒やぎさんから　お手紙　ついた
白やぎさんたら　読まずに　食べた
しかたが　ないので　お手紙　かいた
さっきの　手紙の　ご用事　なぁに

おさるのかごや
作詞者　山上 武夫　　作曲者　海沼 実

エッサ　エッサ　エッサホイ　サッサ
おさるの　かごやだ　ホイサッサ
日暮れの山道　細い道
小田原ちょうちん　ぶらさげて
ソレ　ヤットコドッコイ　ホイサッサ
ホーイ　ホイホイ　ホイサッサ

2003　6 June

日	月	火	水	木	金	土
1	2	3	4	5	6	7
8	9	10	11	12	13	14
15	16	17	18	19	20	21
22	23	24	25	26	27	28
29	30					

2003　9 September

日	月	火	水	木	金	土
	1	2	3	4	5	6
7	8	9	10	11	12	13
14	15	16	17	18	19	20
21	22	23	24	25	26	27
28	29	30				

2003 コムスン むかしのうた カレンダー

- 1月　どじょっこふなっこ
- 2月　鉄道唱歌
- 3月　ゆりかごの歌
- 4月　花
- 5月　おぼろ月夜
- 6月　山羊さんゆうびん
- 7月　かもめの水兵さん
- 8月　おもちゃのマーチ
- 9月　おさるのかごや
- 10月　紅葉
- 11月　待ちぼうけ
- 12月　ペチカ

2003　1 January

日	月	火	水	木	金	土
			1	2	3	4
5	6	7	8	9	10	11
12	13	14	15	16	17	18
19	20	21	22	23	24	25
26	27	28	29	30	31	

ペチカ

2003　12 December

日	月	火	水	木	金	土
	1	2	3	4	5	6
7	8	9	10	11	12	13
14	15	16	17	18	19	20
21	22	23	24	25	26	27
28	29	30	31			

コムスン むかしのうたカレンダー 2003　COMSN Old Song Calendar 2003　JAPAN
高齢者総合介護サービス　Nursing care services
CL: コムスン　COMSN Inc.　CD: 進士多佳子　Takako Sinzi　D: 桐澤美智子　Michiko Kirisawa　I: 進士多佳子／表紙.6.12月　Takako Sinzi / Cover.Jun.Dec. : 桐澤美智子／1.9月　Michiko Kirisawa / Jan.Sep.
DF: コムスン出版局コムスン・プレス　COMSN publication office "COMSN PRESS"　S: コムスン　COMSN Inc.

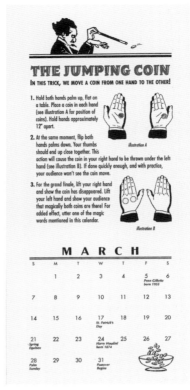

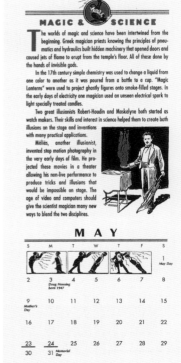

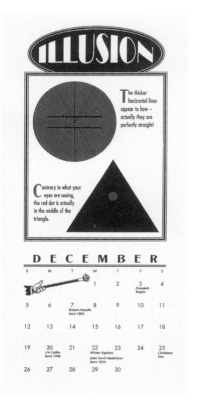

MAGIC&ILLUSION 1999　U.S.A

グラフィックデザイン、写真撮影　Graphic design & Photography

CL: SURFACE Film　　CD, AD, D: Jean Lytle　　AD, CW: Larry Lytle　　DF, S: SURFACE Film

フリックフラック クリスマスカレンダー　Flik Flak Christmas Calendar　2001, 2000　SWITZERLAND
時計メーカー　Watch manufacturer
CL: スウォッチ グループ ジャパン　The Swatch Group (Japan) KK / Swatch Division　　S: スウォッチ グループ ジャパン　The Swatch Group (Japan) KK / Swatch Division

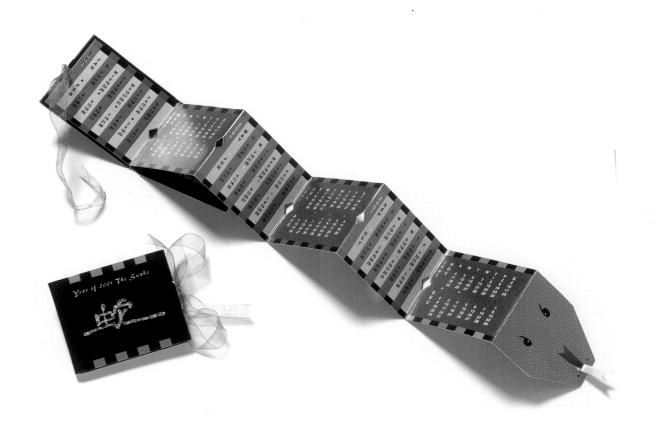

year of rabbit calendar　1999　U.S.A
グラフィックデザイン　Graphic design
CL: JULIA TAM DESIGN　CD, AD, D, I: Julia Chong Tam　DF, S: JULIA TAM DESIGN

year of snake calendar　2001　U.S.A
グラフィックデザイン　Graphic design
CL: JULIA TAM DESIGN　CD, AD, D, I: Julia Chong Tam　DF, S: JULIA TAM DESIGN

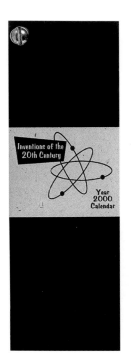

year of horse calendar　2002　U.S.A
グラフィックデザイン　Graphic design
CL: JULIA TAM DESIGN　　CD, AD, D, I: Julia Chong Tam　　DF, S: JULIA TAM DESIGN

INVENTIONS OF THE 20th CENTURY　YEAR 2000　　U.S.A
グラフィックデザイン、写真撮影　Graphic design & Photography
CL: SURFACE Film　　CD, AD, D: Jean Lytle　　AD, CW: Larry Lytle　　DF, S: SURFACE Film

So cool !!　2002　JAPAN

レストラン経営　Restaurant management
CL: ちゃんと　Chanto Co.,Ltd.　Director: 岡田賢一郎　Kenichiro Okada　D: ちゃんと　制作部　Chanto Co.,Ltd. / creative dept.　S: ちゃんと　Chanto Co.,Ltd.

21st. Our Era Meditative Space in The Imaginative Parc
Garden of Gravel and Sand

庭　Garden　2001 JAPAN
菓子製造販売　Confectioners
CL: 長崎堂　Nagasakido co.,ltd.　CD, AD, D, I, Calligrapher: 荒木志華乃　Shigeno Araki　S: 荒木志華乃デザインオフィス　Shigeno Araki Design Office

2003 ランドリー カレンダー　2003 Laundry Calendar　JAPAN
アパレル　Apparel
CL: コラボレーション　Collaboration co.,ltd.　　AD, S: コラボレーション　Collaboration co.,ltd.　　D, I: パンソンワークス　Panson Works

ダイハツ2002企業カレンダー　DAIHATSU 2002 CALENDAR　　JAPAN

自動車の製造　Motor manufacturer
CL: ダイハツ工業　DAIHATSU　CD, AD: 岡田　豊　Yutaka Okada　D: 塩塚美穂　Miho Shiotsuka　P: 柴田一彰　Kazuaki Shibata
DF, S: アートランド・コミュニケーション　ART LAND COMMUNICATION

GOOD MORNING 1997　JAPAN
自動車の製造　Motor manufacturer
CL: トヨタ自動車　TOYOTA　AD, D, I: 駒形克己　Katsumi Komagata　DF, S: ワンストローク　ONE STROKE

紙の卸　Paper merchant

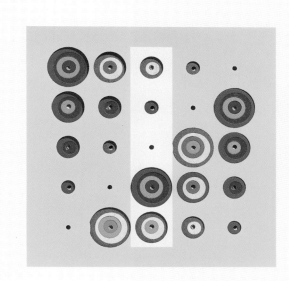

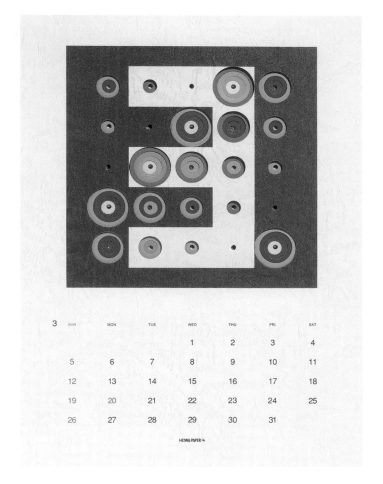

1	SUN	MON	TUE	WED	THU	FRI	SAT
							1
	2	3	4	5	6	7	8
	9	10	11	12	13	14	15
	16	17	18	19	20	21	22
	23/30	24/31	25	26	27	28	29

HEIWA PAPER

3	SUN	MON	TUE	WED	THU	FRI	SAT
				1	2	3	4
	5	6	7	8	9	10	11
	12	13	14	15	16	17	18
	19	20	21	22	23	24	25
	26	27	28	29	30	31	

HEIWA PAPER

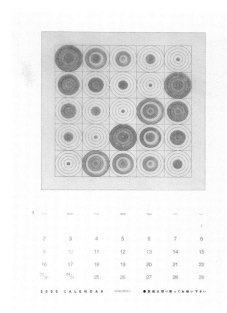

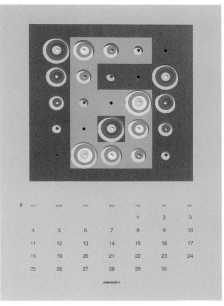

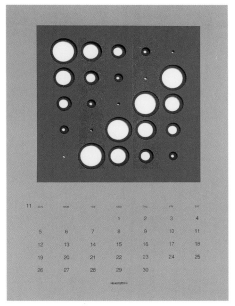

1	SUN	MON	TUE	WED	THU	FRI	SAT
							1
	2	3	4	5	6	7	8
	9	10	11	12	13	14	15
	16	17	18	19	20	21	22
	23/30	24/31	25	26	27	28	29

2000 CALENDAR

6	SUN	MON	TUE	WED	THU	FRI	SAT
					1	2	3
	4	5	6	7	8	9	10
	11	12	13	14	15	16	17
	18	19	20	21	22	23	24
	25	26	27	28	29	30	

HEIWA PAPER

11	SUN	MON	TUE	WED	THU	FRI	SAT
				1	2	3	4
	5	6	7	8	9	10	11
	12	13	14	15	16	17	18
	19	20	21	22	23	24	25
	26	27	28	29	30		

HEIWA PAPER

カラーズ カレンダー　Color's Calendar　2000　JAPAN

紙の卸　Paper merchant
CL: 平和紙業　HEIWA PAPER CO.,LTD.　CD: 岡　信吾　Shingo Oka　AD:DNPメディアクリエイト関西　DNP MEDIA CREATE KANSAI　D: 奥村昭夫　Akio Okumura
DF: パッケージングクリエイト　PACKAGING CREATE　S: 平和紙業　HEIWA PAPER CO.,LTD.

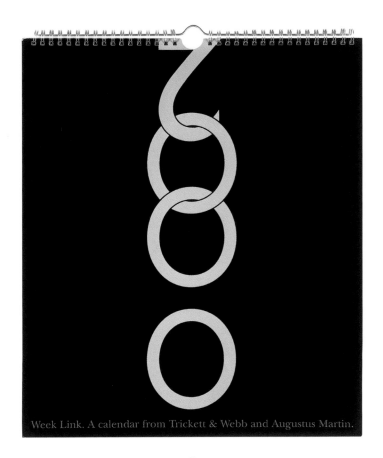

Week Link. A calendar from Trickett & Webb and Augustus Martin.

winter

m	t	w	t	f	s	s
10	11	12	13	14	15	16

JANUARY   Week Link Published by: **Trickett & Webb Ltd** and **Augustus Martin Ltd** Illustration: **John Lawrence**

next

m	t	w	t	f	s	s
31	1	2	3	4	5	6

JAN - FEB   Week Link Published by: **Trickett & Webb Ltd** and **Augustus Martin Ltd** Illustration: **Debbie Cook**

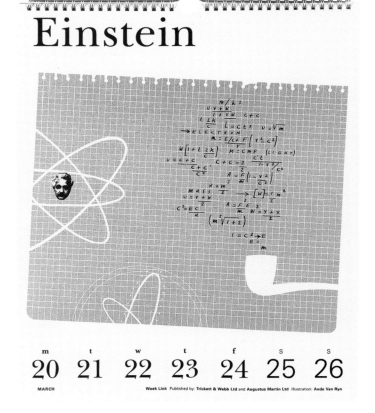

Einstein

m	t	w	t	f	s	s
20	21	22	23	24	25	26

MARCH   Week Link Published by: **Trickett & Webb Ltd** and **Augustus Martin Ltd** Illustration: **Aude Van Ryn**

WEEK LINK   2000 U.K

印刷、デザイン Printers & Designers
CL: AUGUSTUS MARTIN & TRICKETT & WEBB   CD: Lynn Trickett : Brian Webb   D: Heidi Lightfoot   I: George Hardie / on : John Lawrence / winter : Debbie Cook / next : Aude Van Ryn / Einstein : Patrick Thomas / are
: Richard McGuire / this, : Philippe Weisbecker / weeks : Toby Morison / start : Bruce Ingman / zoom   CW: Neil Mattingley   DF, S: TRICKETT & WEBB

are

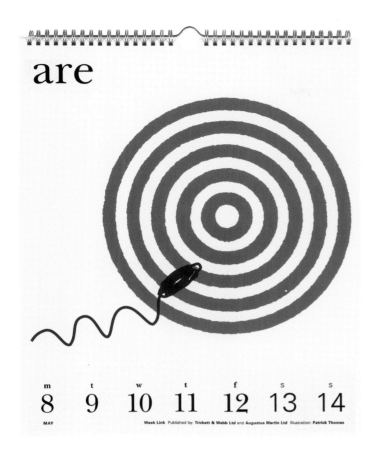

m	t	w	t	f	s	s
8	9	10	11	12	13	14

MAY　　　Week Link Published by: Trickett & Webb Ltd and Augustus Martin Ltd Illustration: Patrick Thomas

weeks

m	t	w	t	f	s	s
3	4	5	6	7	8	9

JULY　　　Week Link Published by: Trickett & Webb Ltd and Augustus Martin Ltd Illustration: Philippe Weisbecker

start

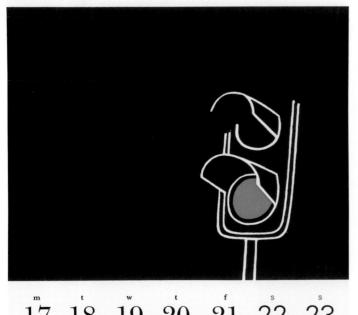

m	t	w	t	f	s	s
17	18	19	20	21	22	23

JULY　　　Week Link Published by: Trickett & Webb Ltd and Augustus Martin Ltd Illustration: Toby Morison

zoom

m	t	w	t	f	s	s
23	24	25	26	27	28	29

OCTOBER　　　Week Link Published by: Trickett & Webb Ltd and Augustus Martin Ltd Illustration: Bruce Ingman

印刷、デザイン　Printers & Designers

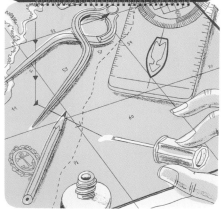

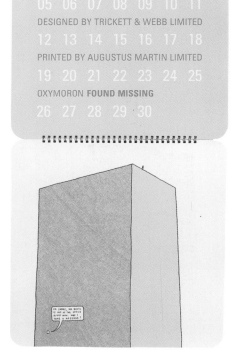

MAY ILLUSTRATED BY ANDRZEJ KLIMOWSKI
DESIGNED BY TRICKETT & WEBB LIMITED
PRINTED BY AUGUSTUS MARTIN LIMITED
OXYMORON **LADY BOY**

NOVEMBER ILLUSTRATED BY TOM GAULD
DESIGNED BY TRICKETT & WEBB LIMITED
PRINTED BY AUGUSTUS MARTIN LIMITED
OXYMORON **FOUND MISSING**

AUGUST ILLUSTRATED BY SARA FANELLI
DESIGNED BY TRICKETT & WEBB LIMITED
PRINTED BY AUGUSTUS MARTIN LIMITED
OXYMORON **DELIBERATE MISTAKE**

OCTOBER ILLUSTRATED BY AUDE VAN RYN
DESIGNED BY TRICKETT & WEBB LIMITED
PRINTED BY AUGUSTUS MARTIN LIMITED
OXYMORON **INSIDE OUT**

I CAN'S STAND SITTING DOWN　2001　U.K

印刷、デザイン　Printers & Designers
CL: AUGUSTUS MARTIN & TRICKETT & WEBB　CD: Lynn Trickett : Brian Webb　D: Matthew Lowe　I: Toby Morison / Jan : Andrzej Klimowski / May : Sara Fanelli / Aug : Aude Van Ryn / Oct : Tom Gauld / Nov
CW: Neil Mattingley　DF, S: TRICKETT & WEBB

PIZZA TO GO　2002　U.K

印刷、デザイン　Printers & Designers
CL: AUGUSTUS MARTIN & TRICKETT & WEBB　CD: Lynn Trickett : Brian Webb　D: Katja Thielen　I: Peter Blake / Jan : Marion Deuchars / Feb : Andrzej Klimowski / Mar : Dan Fern / Jun : Paul Davis / Sep
DF, S: TRICKETT & WEBB

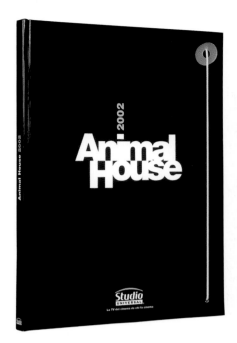

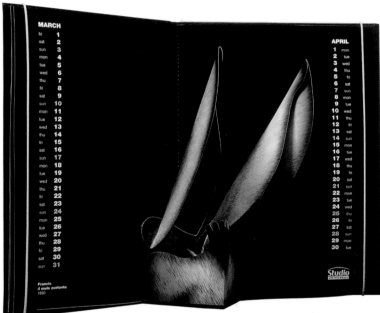

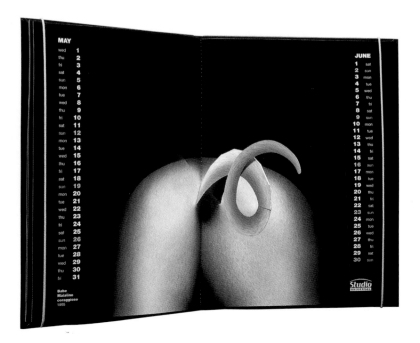

ANIMAL HOUSE　2002　ITALY

映画有料テレビチャンネル　Movie pay TV channel
CL: STUDIO UNIVERSAL　S: UNIVERSAL NETWORKS SERVICES ITALIA SRL

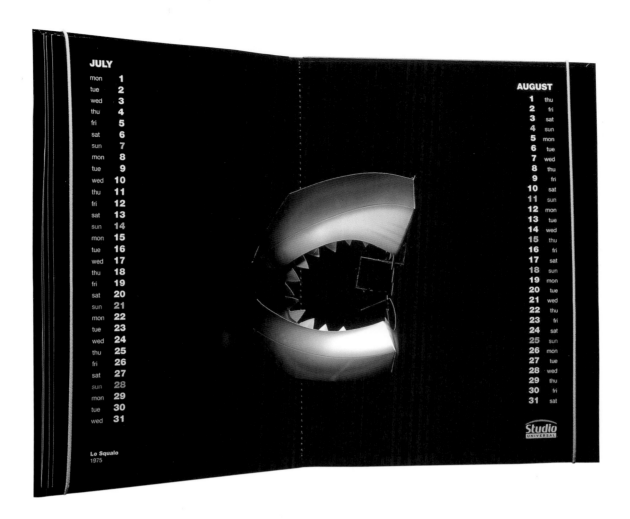

JULY

mon	1
tue	2
wed	3
thu	4
fri	5
sat	6
sun	7
mon	8
tue	9
wed	10
thu	11
fri	12
sat	13
sun	14
mon	15
tue	16
wed	17
thu	18
fri	19
sat	20
sun	21
mon	22
tue	23
wed	24
thu	25
fri	26
sat	27
sun	28
mon	29
tue	30
wed	31

AUGUST

1	thu
2	fri
3	sat
4	sun
5	mon
6	tue
7	wed
8	thu
9	fri
10	sat
11	sun
12	mon
13	tue
14	wed
15	thu
16	fri
17	sat
18	sun
19	mon
20	tue
21	wed
22	thu
23	fri
24	sat
25	sun
26	mon
27	tue
28	wed
29	thu
30	fri
31	sat

Lo Squalo
1975

Studio UNIVERSAL

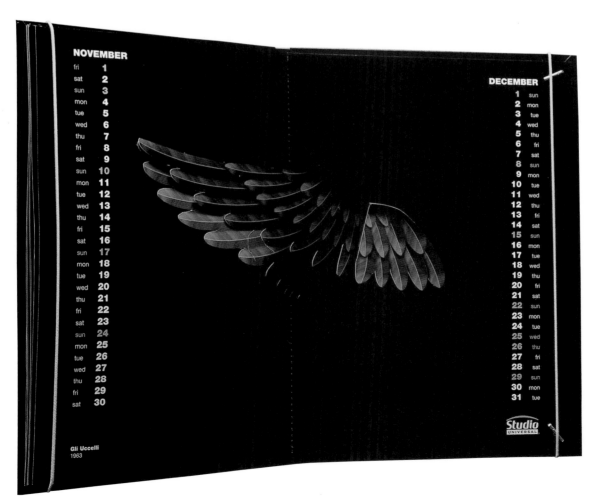

NOVEMBER

fri	1
sat	2
sun	3
mon	4
tue	5
wed	6
thu	7
fri	8
sat	9
sun	10
mon	11
tue	12
wed	13
thu	14
fri	15
sat	16
sun	17
mon	18
tue	19
wed	20
thu	21
fri	22
sat	23
sun	24
mon	25
tue	26
wed	27
thu	28
fri	29
sat	30

DECEMBER

1	sun
2	mon
3	tue
4	wed
5	thu
6	fri
7	sat
8	sun
9	mon
10	tue
11	wed
12	thu
13	fri
14	sat
15	sun
16	mon
17	tue
18	wed
19	thu
20	fri
21	sat
22	sun
23	mon
24	tue
25	wed
26	thu
27	fri
28	sat
29	sun
30	mon
31	tue

Gli Uccelli
1963

Studio UNIVERSAL

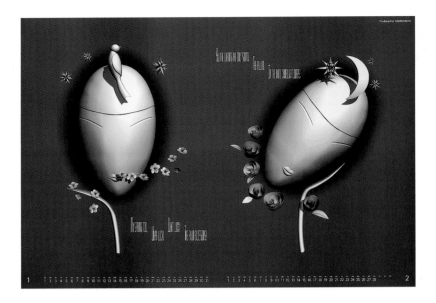

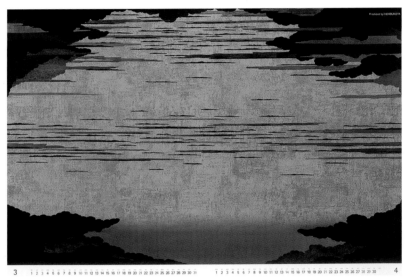

JIPANG:2002 Calendar Designed by 6 Designers in Japanese Traditional Colors
6人のグラフィックデザイナーとプリンティングディレクターとの実験的コラボレーションによる日本の伝統色を使った2002年カレンダー展　JAPAN

印刷　Printer
CL: 研文社　Kenbunsya Co.,Ltd.　CD: リトウ リンダ　Linda Ritoh　AD: リトウ リンダ＋南部俊安　Linda Ritoh+Toshiyasu Nanbu　D: 荒木優子／1.2月　Yuko Araki / Jan.Feb.
: 河本文夫／3.4月　Fumio Kawamoto / Mar.Apr. : シマダ タモツ／5.6月　Tamotsu Shimada / May.Jun. : 南部俊安／7.8月　Toshiyasu Nanbu / Jul.Aug. : 野上周一／9.10月　Shuichi Nogami / Sep.Oct.
: リトウ リンダ／11.12月　Linda Ritoh / Nov.Dec.　CW: リトウ リンダ＋尾鼻和彦　Linda Ritoh+Kazuhiko Obana　S: リビドゥ＆リンダグラフィカ　Libido Inc. & Linda Graphica

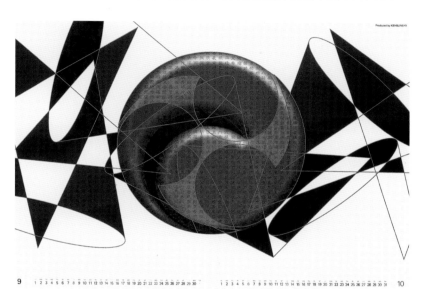

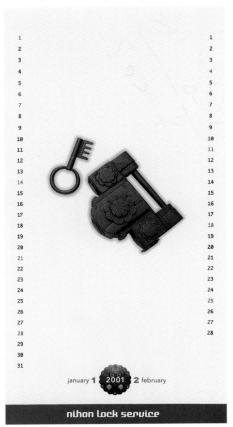

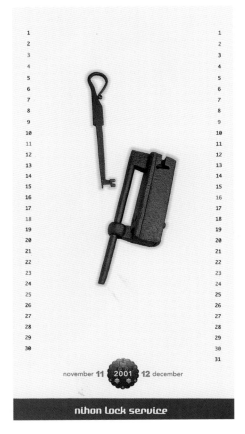

NLS 2001 Calendar　日本ロックサービス2001カレンダー　　JAPAN
防犯グッズの製造・販売、各種ロックの販売・施工　Supplier of crime prevention goods
CL: 日本ロックサービス　nihon lock service　CD: 永田　満／NLS　Mitsuru Nagata／NLS　AD, D: 烏頭尾秀章　Hideaki Utoo　P: 渡辺和宏／スタジオKAZ　Kazuhiro Watanabe／Studio KAZ
DF, S: アラカグラフィス　ALAKA GRAPHIS

Be well informed of the local information.

Maintaining good health is important when travelling abroad.

Never say yes to drugs wherever you are.

外務省 2002 海外安全カレンダー　THE MINISTRY OF FOREIGN AFFAIRS OF JAPAN 2002 CALENDAR　JAPAN

外務省　The ministry of foreign affairs

CL: 外務省　The ministry of foreign affairs　CD, CW: 岩崎竹彦　Takehiko Iwazaki　AD: 永田武史　Takeshi Nagata　D: 太田雄介　Yusuke Ohta：小林洋介　Yosuke Kobayashi：植松晶子　Akiko Uematsu
P: 友野　正　Tadashi Tomono　DF: YOMIKO ADVERTISING INC.　DF, S: E.

1

2002 JANUARY

IHI

SUN	MON	TUE	WED	THU	FRI	SAT
		1	2	3	4	5
6	7	8	9	10	11	12
13	14	15	16	17	18	19
20	21	22	23	24	25	26
27	28	29	30	31		

IHI 2002 Calendar　JAPAN
重機械、造船、鉄鋼、プラントなど　Heavy instruments, Shipbuilding, Steel, Plant
CL: 石川島播磨重工業　Ishikawajima-Harima Heavy Industries Co.,Ltd.　CD, CW: 神谷幸之助　Kounosuke Kamitani　AD, D, I: 塚本明彦　Akihiko Tsukamoto　DF, S: 図案倶楽部　Design Club

4 2002 APRIL	SUN	MON	TUE	WED	THU	FRI	SAT
		1	2	3	4	5	6
	7	8	9	10	11	12	13
	14	15	16	17	18	19	20
	21	22	23	24	25	26	27
IHI	28	29	30				

7 2002 JULY	SUN	MON	TUE	WED	THU	FRI	SAT
		1	2	3	4	5	6
	7	8	9	10	11	12	13
	14	15	16	17	18	19	20
	21	22	23	24	25	26	27
IHI	28	29	30	31			

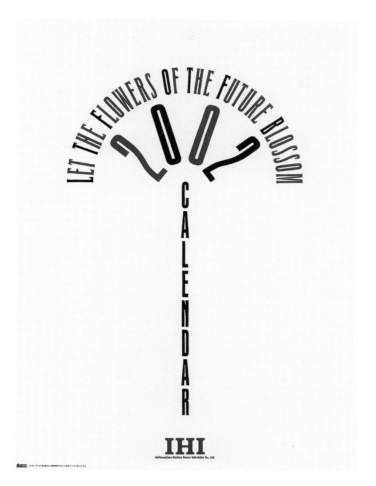

12 2002 DECEMBER	SUN	MON	TUE	WED	THU	FRI	SAT
	1	2	3	4	5	6	7
	8	9	10	11	12	13	14
	15	16	17	18	19	20	21
	22	23	24	25	26	27	28
IHI	29	30	31				

Monet's Garden

モ ネ の 庭

一八八三年の春
モネはパリ郊外
セーヌ川沿いの静かな村、
ジヴェルニーに
移り住んだ。

この地にモネは、
自らの手で
光と色を現出する
理想郷を創りながら、
それを描き続けた。

印象派の、
あのキラキラと
輝く明るい色彩は、
ここから生まれた。

連作八点の総延長は
九一ｍにも及ぶ
モネの集大成「睡蓮」は、
この庭なくしては
表現することは
できなかった。

その睡蓮は、
ここを訪れる人に
無限のインスピレーションを
与え続けている。

5

sunday	monday	tuesday	wednesday	thursday	friday	saturday
			1	2	3	4
5	6	7	8	9	10	11
12	13	14	15	16	17	18
19	20	21	22	23	24	25
26	27	28	29	30	31	

NTT COMWARE
www.nttcom.co.jp

NTTコムウェア 2002カレンダー "奇跡が生まれた場所"　NTT COMWARE 2002 CALENDAR "Places Where Miracle Occurred"　JAPAN

情報通信システムの開発・運用 IT
CL: NTTコムウェア　NTT COMWARE CORPORATION　CD: 池谷　勝　Masaru Ikeya：五ノ井　淳　Jun Gonoi　AD: 清水節江　Setsue Shimizu　CW: こしみず幸三　Kozo Koshimizu
D: 牛尾敏明　Toshiaki Ushio：小嶋隆太　Ryuta kojima　P: 若杉憲司　Kenji Wakasugi　Producer: 住本宣子　Nobuko Sumimoto　DF, S: C' Co.,Ltd.

Helen Keller's Water Pump
ヘレン・ケラーの井戸

4

sunday	monday	tuesday	wednesday	thursday	friday	saturday
	1	2	3	4	5	6
7	8	9	10	11	12	13
14	15	16	17	18	19	20
21	22	23	24	25	26	27
28	29	30				

Wright Brothers' Sky
ライト兄弟の空

1

sunday	monday	tuesday	wednesday	thursday	friday	saturday
		1	2	3	4	5
6	7	8	9	10	11	12
13	14	15	16	17	18	19
20	21	22	23	24	25	26
27	28	29	30	31		

Michelangelo Ceiling
ミケランジェロの天井

12

sunday	monday	tuesday	wednesday	thursday	friday	saturday
1	2	3	4	5	6	7
8	9	10	11	12	13	14
15	16	17	18	19	20	21
22	23	24	25	26	27	28
29	30	31				

奇跡が生まれた場所

Places Where Miracles Occurred

2002 CALENDAR

1

4

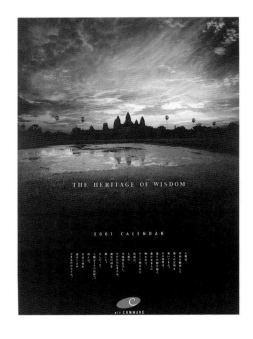

9

10

NTTコムウェア 2001カレンダー「THE HERITAGE OF WISDOM」　NTT COMWARE 2002 CALENDAR「THE HERITAGE OF WISDOM」　JAPAN
情報通信システムの開発・運用　IT
CL: NTTコムウェア NTT COMWARE CORPORATION　CD: 池谷　勝 Masaru Ikeya：五ノ井　淳 Jun Gonoi　AD: 清水節江 Setsue Shimizu　CW: こしみず幸三 Kozo Koshimizu
D: 佐藤　郁 Iku Sato：中村直美 Naomi Nakamura　P: 帆足侊兀 Terutaka Hoashi　Producer: 住本宣子 Nobuko Sumimoto　DF, S: C' Co.,Ltd.

四季華景色　Flower Scenes in Four Seasons　2003　JAPAN
写真エージェンシー　Photograph agency
CL: 丹溪　TANKEI Co.,LTD.　CD, AD, P: 前田　晃　Akira Maeda　D: 白谷敏夫　Toshio Shiratani　DF: ノマド　NOMADE　S: 丹溪　TANKEI Co.,LTD.

2001 ROMANDO & HIDEOKI CALENDAR　JAPAN
広告企画制作　A full-service advertising agency
CL: 浪漫堂　Romando co.,ltd.　CD, AD, D: 生駒由紀夫　Yukio Ikoma　P: 英興　Hideoki　DF, S: アイム　I'm co.,ltd.

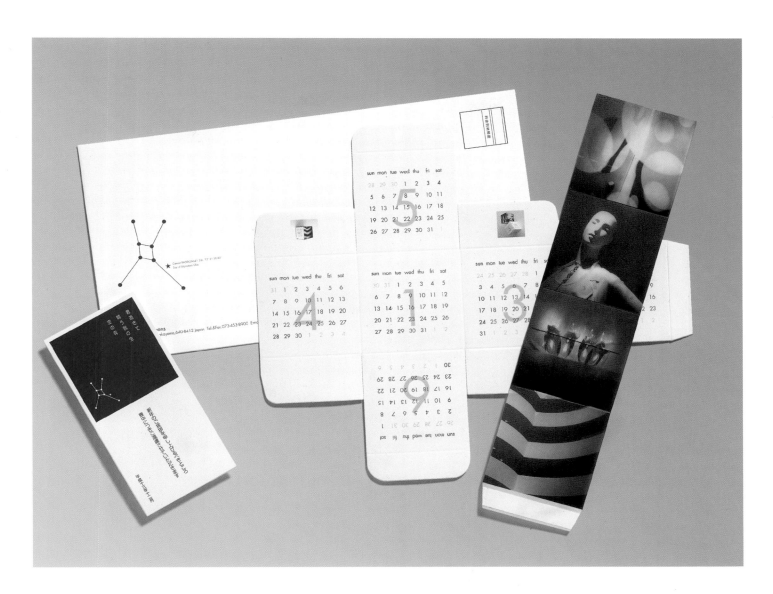

岡 桃太郎の星　Star of Momotaro Oka　2002　JAPAN
デザイン事務所　Design firm
CL: デザインユニット リ・ビーンズ　Design Unit Re Beans　　AD, P: 岡 記生　Norio Oka　　D, CW: 岡 公美　Kumi Oka　　S: デザインユニット リ・ビーンズ　Design Unit Re Beans

世界遺産 琉球王国 WORLD HERITAGE　RYUKYU KINGDOM　2002 JAPAN
移動通信サービス Mobile communications service
CL: NTTドコモ九州 NTT DoCoMo KYUSHU　CD: 桑原庄司 Syoji Kuwahara　AD: 伊藤敬生 Takao Ito　P: 知識たかし Takashi Chishiki　D: 鈴木理恵子 Rieko Suzuki　CW: 水島理恵 Rie Mizushima
Coordinator: ロケーションファースト LOCATION FIRST　DF: NTTアド NTT AD　AD: 電通九州 DENTSU KYUSHU　アド・パスカル AD PASCAL　S: 電通九州 DENTSU KYUSYU

田中麗奈＋世界遺産琉球王国　RENA TANAKA IN OKINAWA THE WORLD HERITAGE NTT DoCoMo KYUSHU 2002 CALENDAR　JAPAN

移動通信サービス　Mobile communications service
CL: NTTドコモ九州　NTT DoCoMo KYUSHU　CD: 桑原庄司　Syoji Kuwahara　AD: 伊藤敬生　Takao Ito　D: 鈴木理恵子　Rieko Suzuki　P: 知識たかし　Takashi Chishiki　CW: 水島理恵　Rie Mizushima
Stylist: 吉野輝脩　Yosuke Yoshino　Hairmake: 渡辺真由美　Mayumi Watanabe　Coordinator: ロケーションファースト　LOCATION FIRST　DF: NTTアド　NTT AD：電通九州　DENTSU KYUSYU
：アド・パスカル　AD PASCAL　S: 電通九州　DENTSU KYUSYU

Konno Chuichi 2000 Calendar-Ages of Mankind-　JAPAN

美術商　Fine art quotient
CL: トゥレス　Torres Inc.　CD: 今野怜子　Reiko Konno　AD: 原　耕一　Koichi Hara　D: 渡邊隆雄　Takao Watanabe　P: 宮澤正明　Masaaki Miyazawa　Artist: 今野忠一　Chuichi Konno
DF, S: トラウト　Trout Inc.

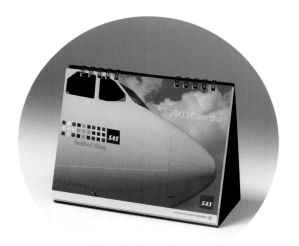

SAS 2003 CALENDAR　スカンジナビア航空 2003年カレンダー　JAPAN

運輸業　Transportation
CL: スカンジナビア航空　Scandinavian Airlines System　　S: スカンジナビア航空　Scandinavian Airlines System

1982

⑦	⑧	⑨	⑩	⑪	⑫

1982

❶	❷	❸	❹	❺	❻

'82東芝海外向けTVカレンダー '82 TOSHIBA TV calendar for the foreign countries　JAPAN

家電　Home electrics
CL: 東芝　TOSHIBA　CD: 高木基広　Motohiro Takagi　AD, D: 井山高秀　Takahide Iyama　I: 松井伸佳　Nobuyoshi Matui　DF: デコス　Decos　S: デザイン プロット スタジオ　Design Plot Studio inc.

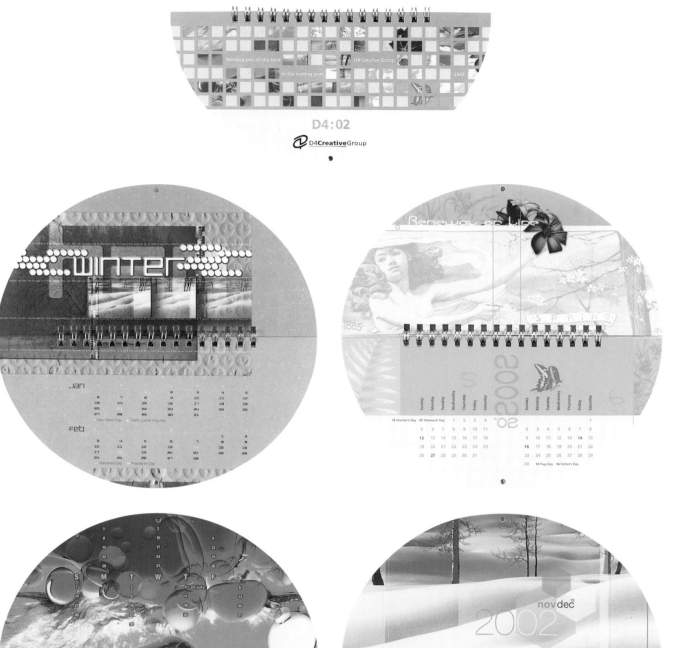

D4 CREATIVE GROUP 2001-2002 CALENDAR   U.S.A

広告代理店 Advertising agency
CL: D4 CREATIVE GROUP   AD, I: Wicky Lee : Ian Brand : Andrew Snyder : Tara James   D, I: Cesar Varela   D: Shawn Muldowney   DF, S: D4 CREATIVE GROUP

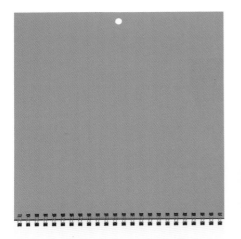

every new year
brings many new
days. here is a list of
all the ones you can
look forward to

welcome the feeling of refreshed spirit

take a fantastic voyage

feel funny

come to terms
with dangerous passions

eat my saliva

leap out gently

Fly CALENDAR　2001 U.K
グラフィックデザイン　Graphic design
CL: Fly　　AD, P: Fabian Monheim　　AD, P, CW: Sophia Wood　　S: Fly

RIORDON 2002 CALENDAR　CANADA

グラフィックデザイン事務所　Graphic design firm
CL: The Riordon Design Group　　CD: Dan Wheaton　　AD, P: Ric Riordon　　D: Amy Montgomery : Sharon Pece : Shirley Riordon　　P: Stock Image　　I: Tim Warnock(for letter press image on box)　　CW: QUOTES
DF, S: The Riordon Design Group

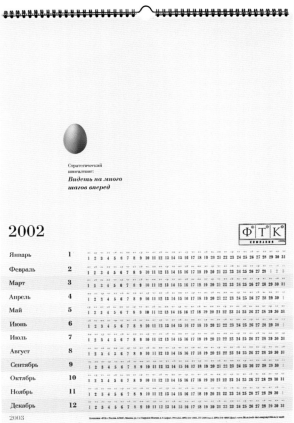

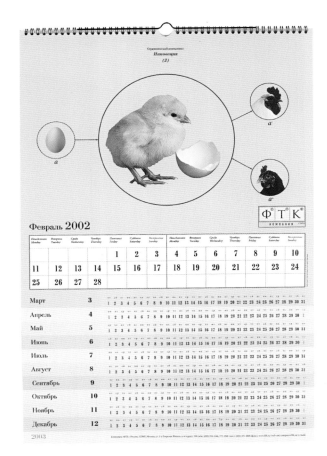

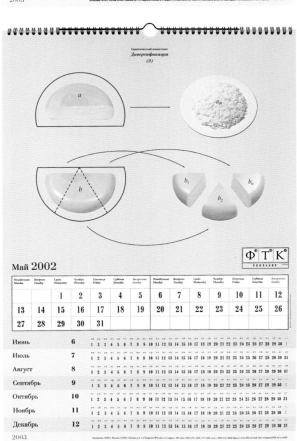

FTC 2002　RUSSIA
経営コンサルタント　Financial consulting
CL: FTC　CD, D: Kuzhavsky Sergei　AD: Jitzky Stas　P: Martyakhin Sergei　DF, S: OPEN ! DESIGN & CONCEPTS

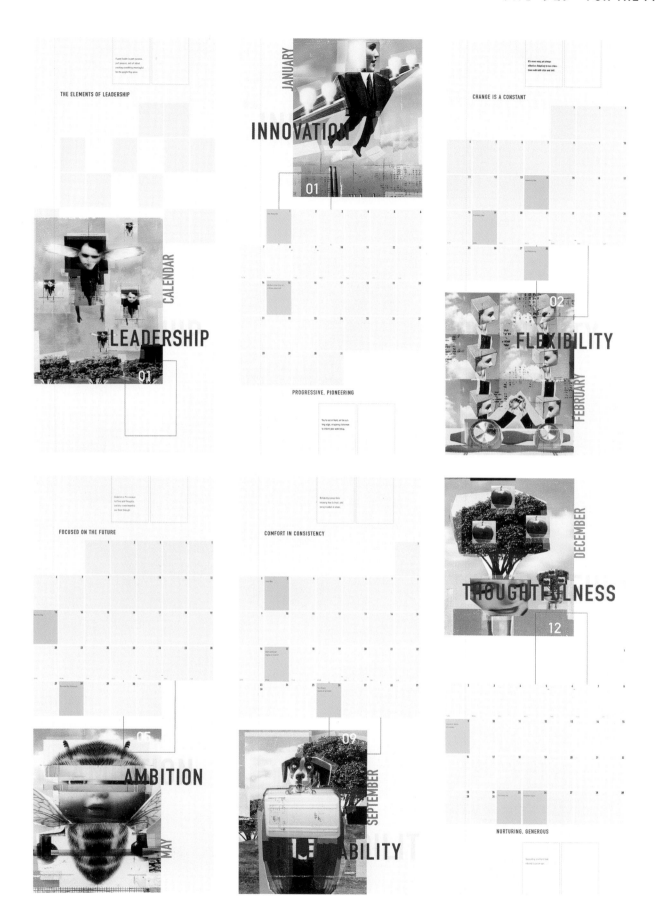

PEAKE CALENDAR　2001　U.S.A

印刷　Printer
CL: PEAKE PRINTERS　D: Sam Shelton : Jeff Fabian : Beth Clawson : Beverley Hunter : Ali Kooistra : Katie Kroener : Kamomi Solidum : Scott Rier　DF: KINETIK
S: KINETIK COMMUNICATION GRAPHICS,INC.

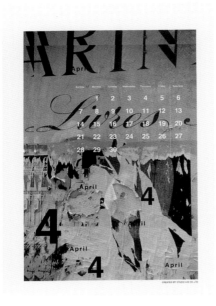

スタジオ ビス オリジナルカレンダー　studio vis ORIGINAL CALENDAR　2002 JAPAN
広告企画制作　A full-service advertising agency
CL: スタジオ ビス　studio vis co.,ltd.　CD, D: 草次耕二　Koji Kusatsugu　S: スタジオ ビス　studio vis co.,ltd.

スタジオ ビス オリジナルカレンダー　studio vis ORIGINAL CALENDAR　2000　JAPAN
広告企画制作　A full-service advertising agency
CL: スタジオ ビス　studio vis co.,ltd.　　CD, D: 草次耕二　Koji Kusatsugu　S: スタジオ ビス　studio vis co.,ltd.

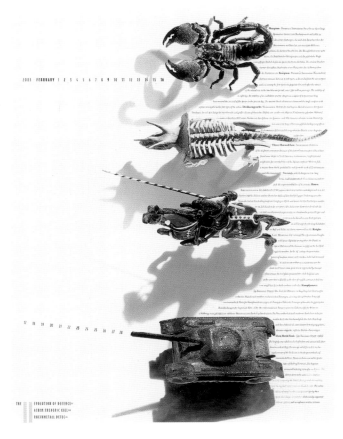

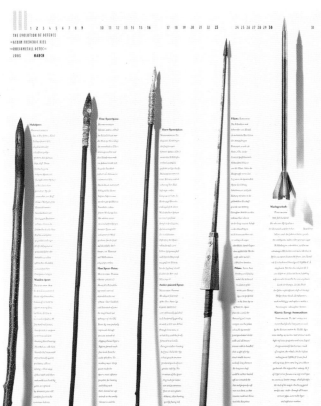

The Evolution of Defence　2003　GERMANY

製造業 Defence technology

CL: Rheinmetall DeTec AG　CD, D: Achim Frederic Kiel　Producer: Reprotechnik Vogel & Partner　P: Thomas Liebig　CW: Delia Partridge　DF, S: Pencil Fine Art

CALENDAR 1998　SWITZERLAND

保険会社　Insurance
CL: HANGAR 21　CD, I: Claudia Meythaler　P: Tiarin E.Wenger　DF, S: 9D DESIGN

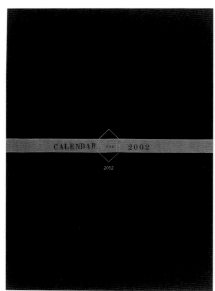
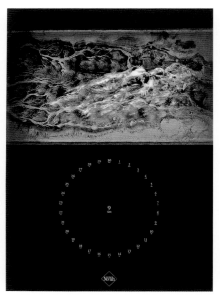

CALENDAR 2002　JAPAN

商業写真及び広告写真全般　Commerce, Advertising photograph studio

CL: スタジオ ノア　Studio No・ah Co.,Ltd.　CD, AD, P: 野波　浩 Hiroshi Nonami　D: 田中克幸　Katsuyuki Tanaka : 石井　敦　Atsushi Ishii　Stylist,Hairmake: 内田百合香　Yurika Uchida
DF: ケイ プラント　K Plant Co.,Ltd.　S: スタジオ ノア　Studio No・ah Co.,Ltd.

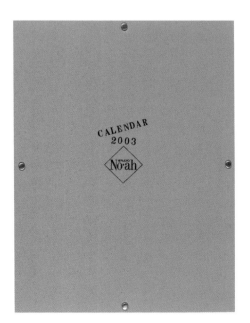

CALENDAR 2003　JAPAN

商業写真及び広告写真全般　Commerce, Advertising photograph studio

CL: スタジオ ノア　Studio No·ah Co.,Ltd.　　CD, AD, P: 野波 浩 Hiroshi Nonami　D: 田中克幸 Katsuyuki Tanaka : 小嶌大介 Daisuke Kojima　Stylist,Hairmake: 内田百合香　Yurika Uchida
DF: ケイ プラント　K Plant Co.,Ltd.　S: スタジオ ノア　Studio No·ah Co.,Ltd.

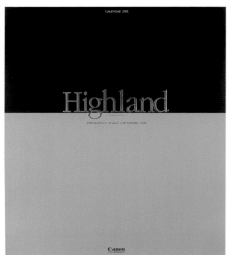

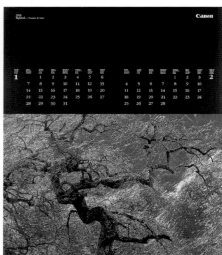

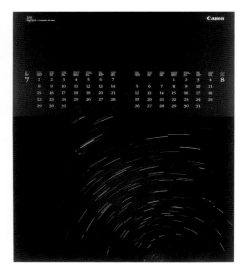

Highland 息吹　2001　JAPAN

商業 Commerce
CL: キヤノン販売　CANON SALES CO.,INC.　CD, AD, D: 内田靖通　Yasumichi Uchida　D: 小日向　誠　Makoto Obinata　P: 吉野　信　Shin Yoshino　S: 凸版印刷　TOPPAN PRINTING CO.,LTD.

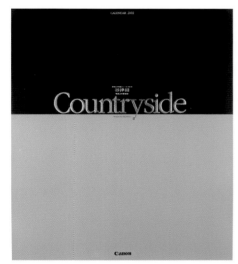

Countryside 谷津田　2002 JAPAN

商業 Commerce
CL: キヤノン販売　CANON SALES CO.,INC.　CD, AD, D: 内田靖通　Yasumichi Uchida　D: 小日向　誠　Makoto Obinata　P: 中野耕志　Koji Nakano　S: 凸版印刷　TOPPAN PRINTING CO.,LTD.

いちごの旅　The travel of strawberry　2002　JAPAN

いちごの旅　The travel of strawberry　2002　JAPAN
生命保険会社　Life insurance
CL: プルデンシャル生命保険会社　Prudential life office　　CD, CW: 鈴木猛之　Takeshi Suzuki　　AD: 永田武史　Takeshi Nagata　　D, P: 柴牟田興輔　Kosuke Shimuta　　D: 小林洋介　Yosuke Kobayashi　　DF, S: E.
DF: paradox creative

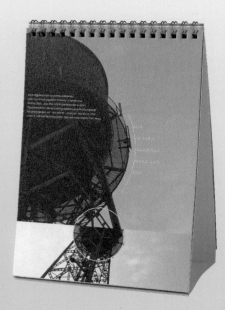

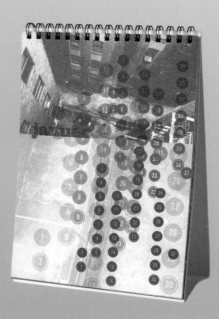

Calendar 2000　GERMANY
写真撮影、グラフィックデザイン　Photographer & Graphic designer
CL: Nielinger & Rohsiepe　CD, AD, P: Christian Nielinger　CD, AD, D: Herbert Rohsiepe　DF, S: Nielinger & Rohsiepe

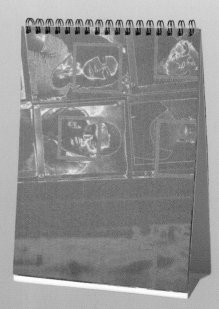
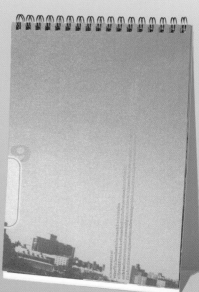

Calendar 2001　GERMANY

写真撮影、グラフィックデザイン　Photographer & Graphic designer
CL: Nielinger & Rohsiepe　CD, AD, P: Christian Nielinger　CD, AD, D: Herbert Rohsiepe　CW: Dr.Ruediger Striemer　DF, S: Nielinger & Rohsiepe

VIVAYOU Spring & Summer '98 CATALOG　JAPAN
アパレル　Apparel
CL: VIVAYOU　AD: 文屋宏隆　Hirotaka Bunya　P: Anette Aurell　S: VIVAYOU

3 march

6 june

2002
Calendar
by DESPERADO & RYUKO TSUSHIN

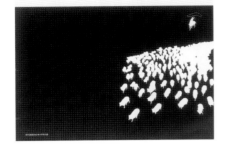

2002 Calendar by DESPERADO & RYUKO TSUSHIN　2002カレンダー　デスペラード＆流行通信　JAPAN

出版　Publisher
CL: インファス　INFAS　CD: 流行通信　RYUKO TSUSHIN : デスペラード　DESPERADO　AD: 小林　恭＋マナ／ima　Takashi Kobayashi+mana / ima　D: 石岡良治　Ryoji Ishioka　P: 安斎重男　Shigeo Anzai
DF: エナメル　enamel　S: ルック　LOOK inc.

CALENDRIER mod's hair　モッズ・ヘア カレンダー　1999 JAPAN
美容業　Beauty salon business
CL: モッズ・ヘア　mod's hair　AD: 高田正治　Masaharu Takata　D: 茂野千里　Chisato Shigeno　P: Nathalie Demontes　DF: タカタデザイン　TAKATA DESIGN　S: モッズ・ヘア　mod's hair

CALENDRIER mod's hair モッズ・ヘア カレンダー　2000　JAPAN

美容業　Beauty salon business
CL: モッズ・ヘア　mod's hair　AD: 高田正治　Masaharu Takata　D: 茂野千里　Chisato Shigeno　P: Nathalie Demontes　DF: タカタデザイン　TAKATA DESIGN　S: モッズ・ヘア　mod's hair

CALENDRIER mod's hair　モッズ・ヘア カレンダー　2003　JAPAN
美容業　Beauty salon business
CL: モッズ・ヘア　mod's hair　AD: 高田正治　Masaharu Takata　D: 茂野千里　Chisato Shigeno　P: Nathalie Demontes　DF: タカタデザイン　TAKATA DESIGN　S: モッズ・ヘア　mod's hair

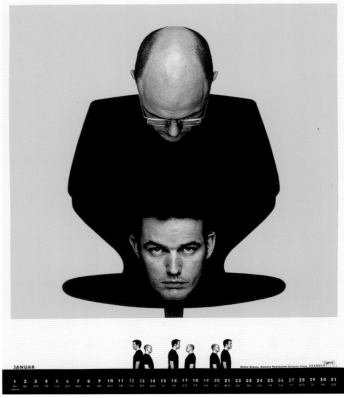

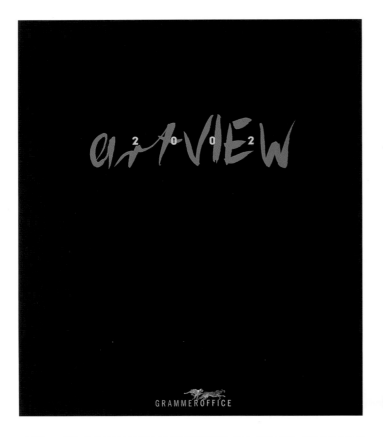

ARTVIEW -GRAMMER OFFICE　2002 GERMANY
椅子の製造 Seat manufacturer
CL: GRAMMER OFFICE　CD: Wilhelm Koch　AD: Manfred Wilhelm : Gerhard Schmidt　D: Josef Grillmeier　P: Erich Spahn　DF, S: BÜRO WILHELM. KOMMUNIKATION UND GESTALTUNG

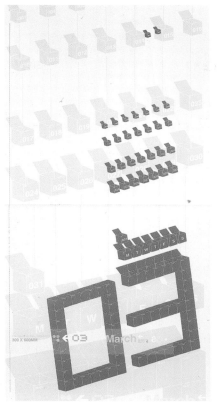

D.M.Steele Eclectic Calendar 2003　　U.S.A

デザイン事務所　Design firm
CL: D.M.Steele Company　S: D.M.Steele Company

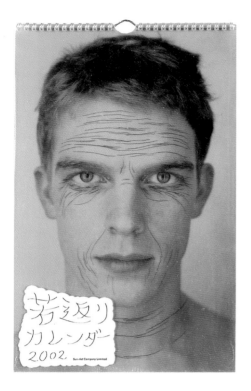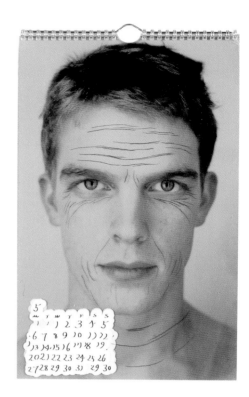

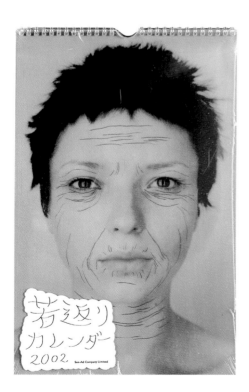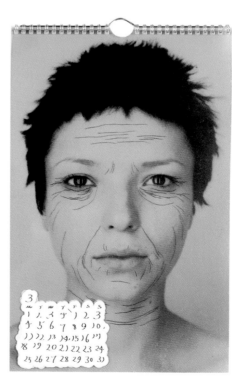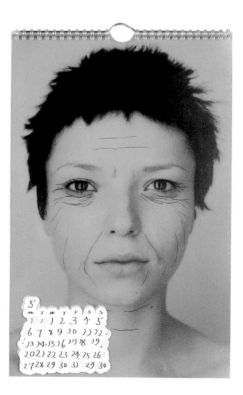

若返りカレンダー　REJUVENATION CALENDAR　2002 JAPAN

広告プロダクション　AD Production

CL: サン・アド　SUN-AD CO.,LTD.　AD: 野田 凪 Nagi Noda　D: 戸田かおり　Kaori Toda　P: 瀧本幹也　Mikiya Takimoto　DF, S: サン・アド　SUN-AD CO.,LTD.

透明フィルムに数字玉とシワを印刷。めくるごとにシワの数が少なくなり、若返っていく仕組み
Number beads and wrinkles printed on transparent film. The wrinkles decrease — representing restoration of youth — with each turn of the page.

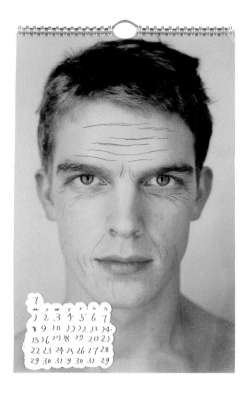
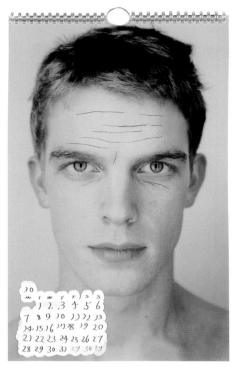
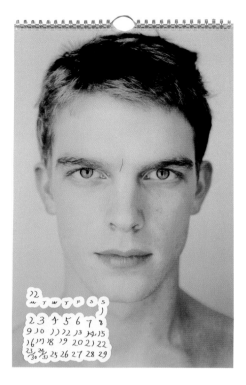

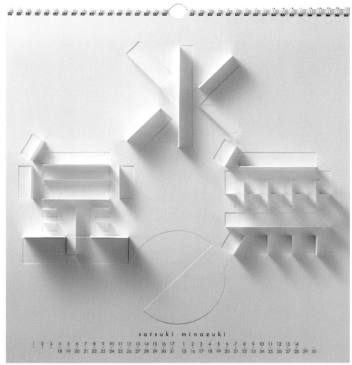

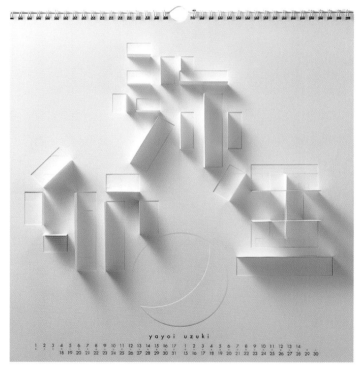

平和ノ和 heiwa no wa 2002 JAPAN

デザイン事務所 Design firm
CL: 左合ひとみデザイン室 Hitomi Sago Design Office,Inc.　AD, D: 左合ひとみ Hitomi Sago　CW: 飯田有貴 Yuki Iida　DF, S: 左合ひとみデザイン室 Hitomi Sago Design Office,Inc.

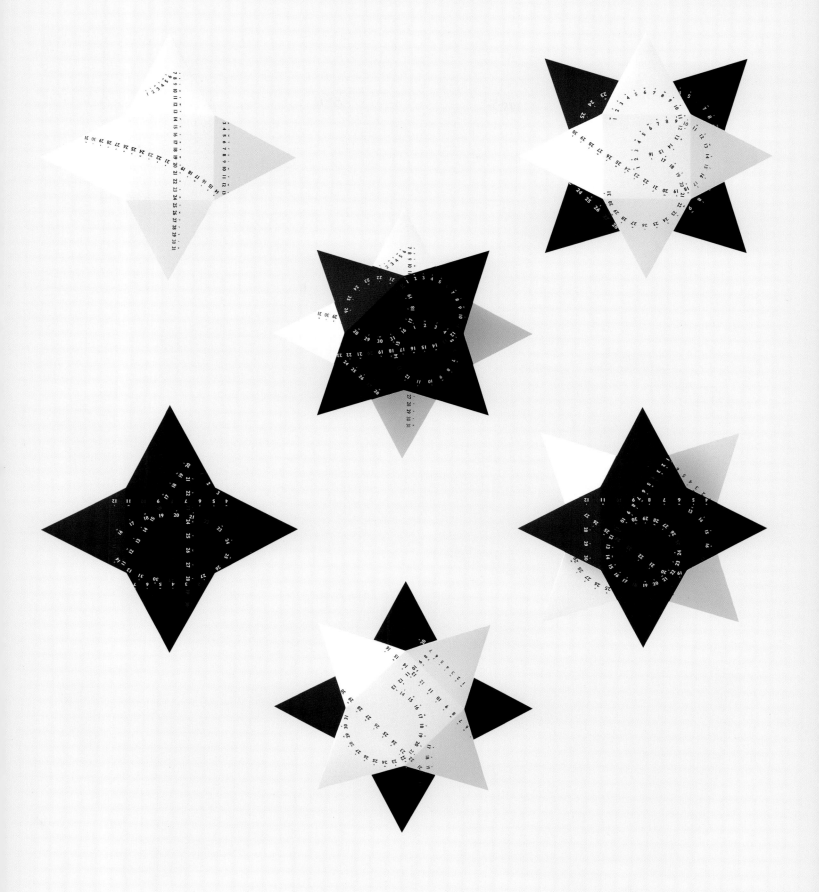

BLACK+WHITE　2000　JAPAN
デザイン事務所　Design firm
CL: 左合ひとみデザイン室　Hitomi Sago Design Office,Inc.　　AD, D: 左合ひとみ　Hitomi Sago　　DF, S: 左合ひとみデザイン室　Hitomi Sago Design Office,Inc.

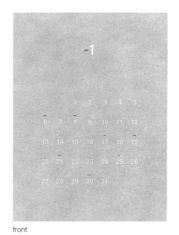

front

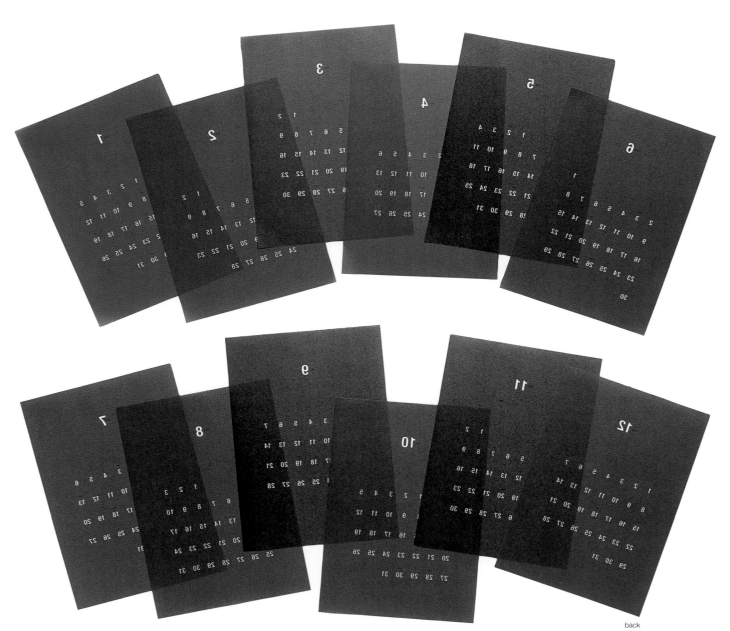

back

Comfortable Component Package Calendar 2002 JAPAN
エヌビー＆ビーキュー **NB & BQ**
CL: 47会 yon-nana kai AD, D: 水野 学 Manabu Mizuno S: グッドデザインカンパニー good design company

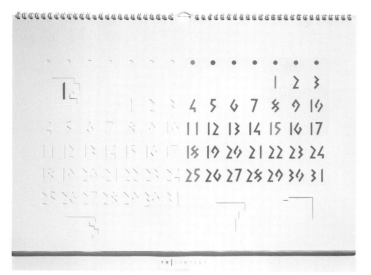

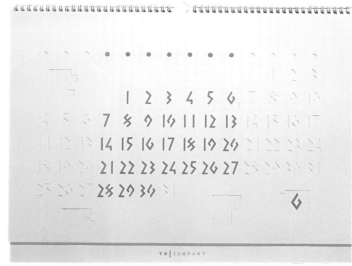

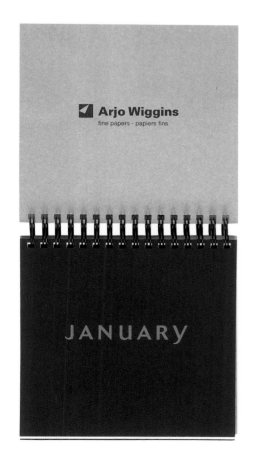

1998 Calendar　JAPAN
印刷　Printer
CL: トライカンパニー　TRI company limited　AD, D: 塚本明彦　Akihiko Tsukamoto　DF, S: 図案倶楽部　Design Club

デスクカレンダー　Desk Calendar　1999 JAPAN
製紙　Paper manufacturer
CL: アルジョ ウィギンス キャンソン　Arjo Wiggins Canson KK　AD, D: 塚本明彦　Akihiko Tsukamoto　DF, S: 図案倶楽部　Design Club

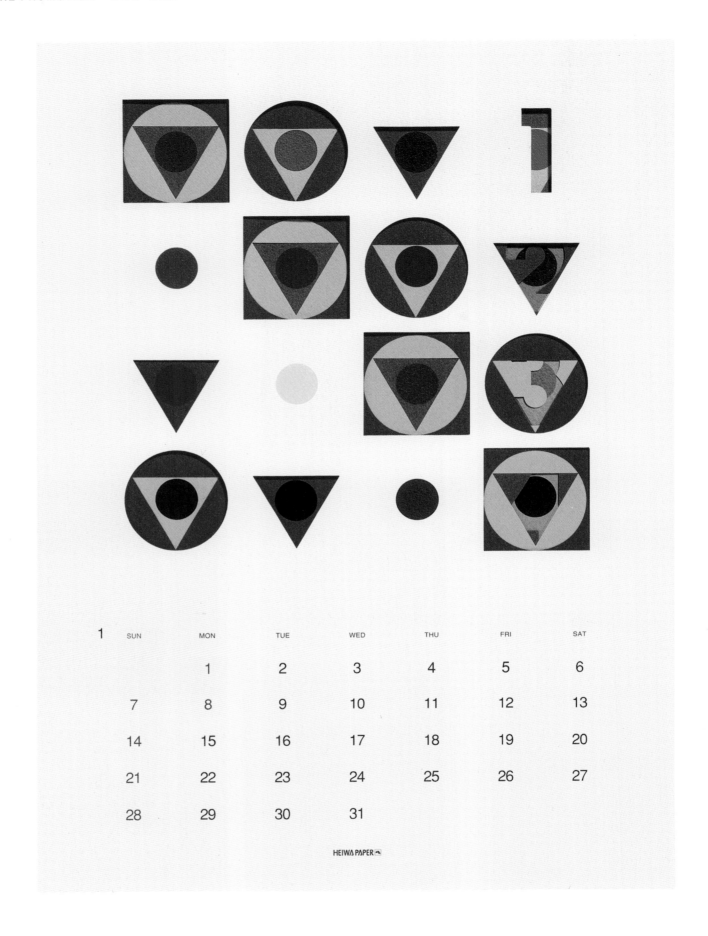

1	SUN	MON	TUE	WED	THU	FRI	SAT
		1	2	3	4	5	6
	7	8	9	10	11	12	13
	14	15	16	17	18	19	20
	21	22	23	24	25	26	27
	28	29	30	31			

HEIWA PAPER

カラーズ カレンダー Color's Calendar　2001　JAPAN

紙の卸　Paper merchant
CL: 平和紙業　HEIWA PAPER CO.,LTD.　CD: 岡　信吾　Shingo Oka　AD: DNPメディアクリエイト関西　DNP MEDIA CREATE KANSAI　D: 奥村昭夫　Akio Okumura
DF: パッケージングクリエイト　PACKAGING CREATE　S: 平和紙業　HEIWA PAPER CO.,LTD.

2001 CALENDAR　HEIWA PAPER㈱　●表紙は切り取ってお使い下さい

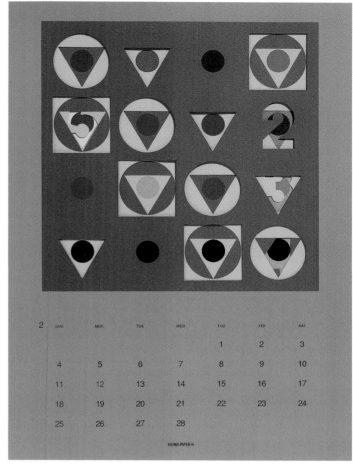

2	SUN	MON	TUE	WED	THU	FRI	SAT
					1	2	3
	4	5	6	7	8	9	10
	11	12	13	14	15	16	17
	18	19	20	21	22	23	24
	25	26	27	28			

HEIWA PAPER㈱

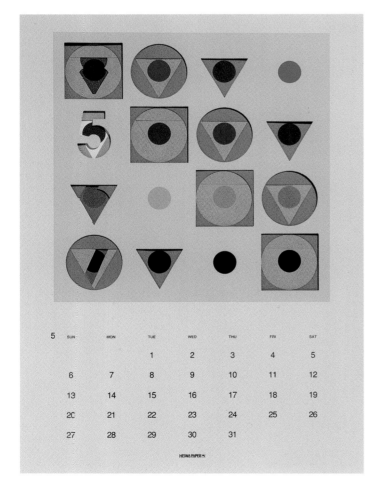

5	SUN	MON	TUE	WED	THU	FRI	SAT
			1	2	3	4	5
	6	7	8	9	10	11	12
	13	14	15	16	17	18	19
	20	21	22	23	24	25	26
	27	28	29	30	31		

HEIWA PAPER㈱

10	SUN	MON	TUE	WED	THU	FRI	SAT
		1	2	3	4	5	6
	7	8	9	10	11	12	13
	14	15	16	17	18	19	20
	21	22	23	24	25	26	27
	28	29	30	31			

HEIWA PAPER㈱

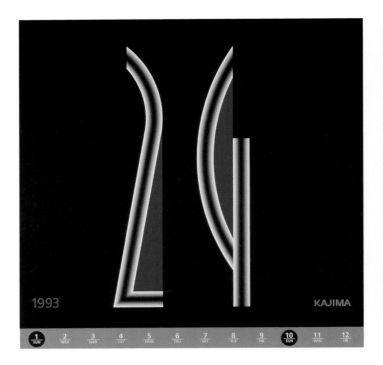

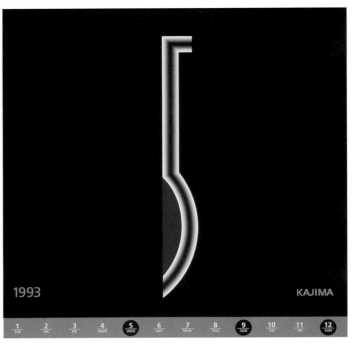

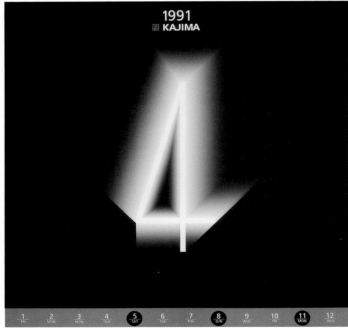

Kajima Daily Calendar 1993　1993年 鹿島 日めくりカレンダー　JAPAN
建設　Construction & Engineering
CL: 鹿島建設　Kajima Corporation　AD, D: 勝井三雄　Mitsuo Katsui　D: 麻生隆一　Ryuichi Aso　DF, S: 勝井デザイン事務所　Katsui Design Office

Kajima Daily Calendar 1991　1991年 鹿島 日めくりカレンダー　JAPAN
建設　Construction & Engineering
CL: 鹿島建設　Kajima Corporation　AD, D: 勝井三雄　Mitsuo Katsui　D: 白井晴美　Harumi Shirai　DF, S: 勝井デザイン事務所　Katsui Design Office

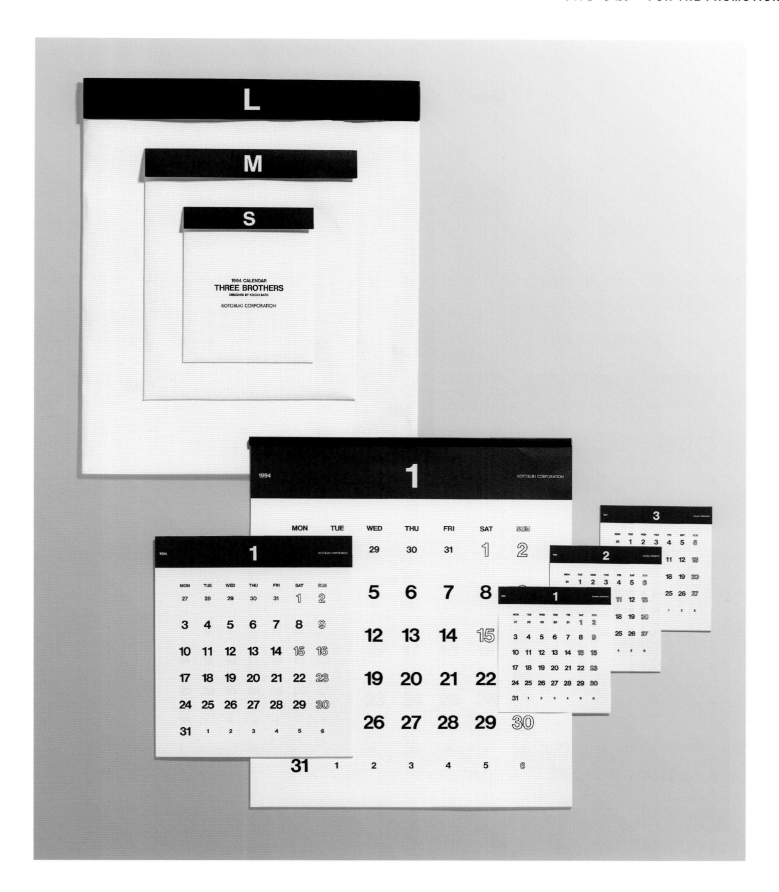

THREE BROTHERS 1994　JAPAN
家具メーカー　Furniture manufacturer
CL: コトブキ　KOTOBUKI CORPORATION　AD, D, S: 佐藤晃一　Koichi Sato

日本の色　2001 calendar Colors of Nippon　JAPAN
2005年日本国際博覧会協会　Japan Association for the 2005 world Exposition
CL: 2005年日本国際博覧会協会　Japan Association for the 2005 world Exposition　CD, AD: 大貫卓也　Takuya Onuki　D: 岸　和弘　Kazuhiro Kishi　S: 大貫デザイン　Onuki DESIGN

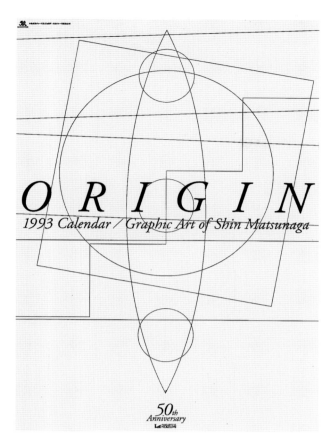

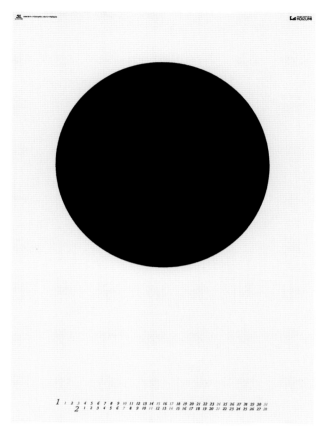

ORIGIN　1993　JAPAN

照明事業、家具事業　Lighting & Furniture business
CL: 小泉産業　KOIZUMI SANGYO CORP.　AD, D: 松永　真　Shin Matsunaga　S: 松永真デザイン事務所　Shin Matsunaga Design Inc.

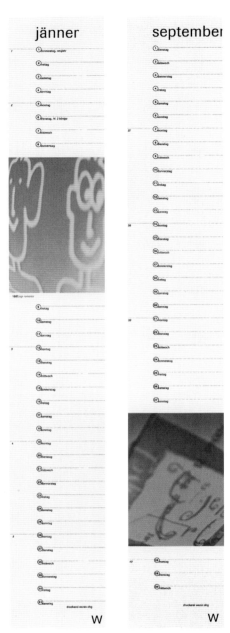

WENIN CALENDARS　2002,2001,1999,1998　AUSTRIA
印刷　Printer
CL: DRUCKEREI WENIN KG　CD, AD: Sigi Ramoser　D: Marcel Schrattner : Klaus Österle　Calligrapher: Hertha Spiegel　DF, S: SÄGENVIER

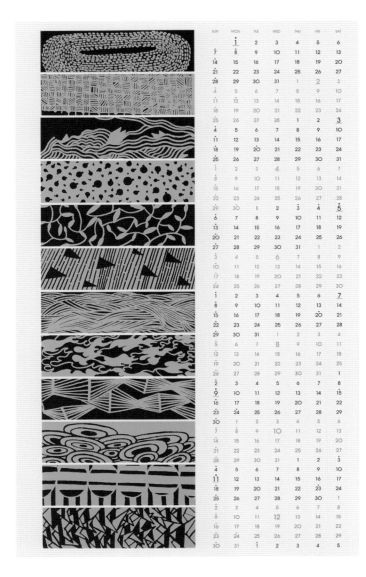

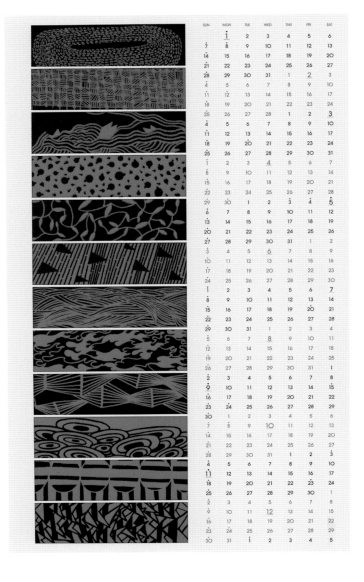

2002 Calendar　JAPAN

デザイン事務所　Design firm
CL: シューデザイン　Chou Design Co.,Ltd.　　AD, D, I: 寒河江亘太　Kouta Sagae　S: シューデザイン　Chou Design Co.,Ltd.

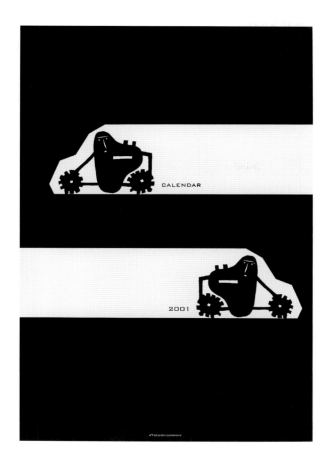

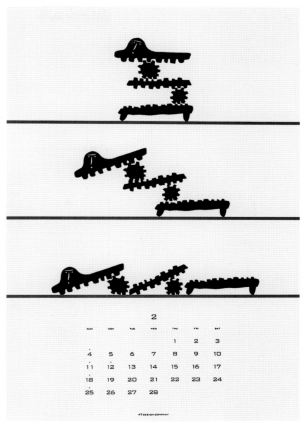

47 design calendar　2001　JAPAN
デザイン事務所　Design firm
CL: 47 design company　AD, I, S: 福田　航　Ko Fukuda

Shiseido WORD Calendar　資生堂・ワード・カレンダー　2003　JAPAN
化粧品メーカー　Cosmetics company
CL: 資生堂　Shiseido　CD: 村上博美　Hiromi Murakami　AD, S: 仲條正義　Masayoshi Nakajo

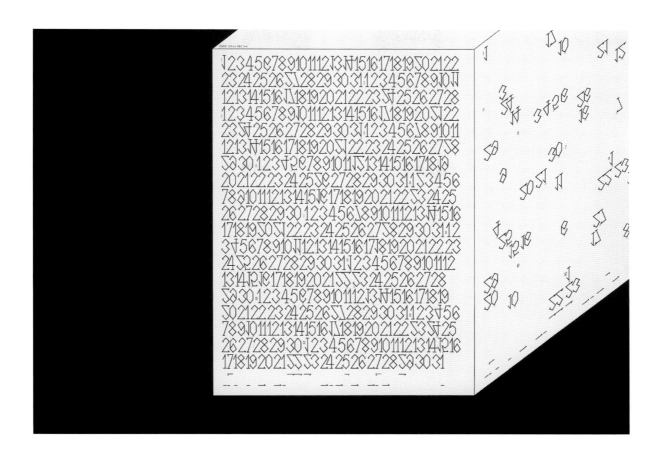

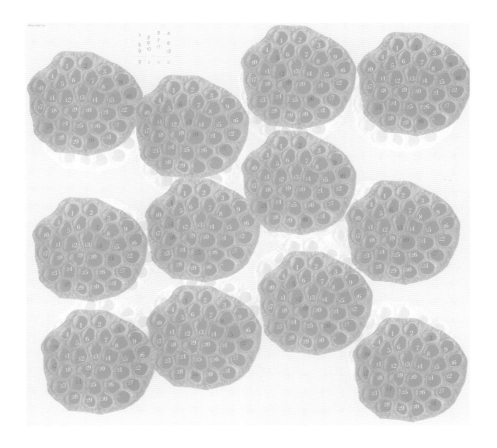

オフィス・ピーアンドシー カレンダー **Office P&C CALENDAR** 2002,2000 JAPAN
デザイン事務所　Design firm
CL: オフィス・ピーアンドシー　Office P&C　AD, D: 八木健夫　Tateo Yagi　S: オフィス・ピーアンドシー　Office P&C

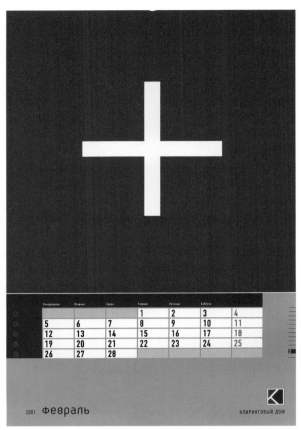

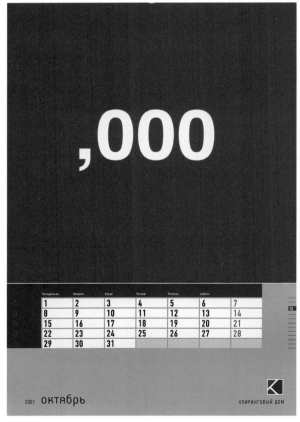

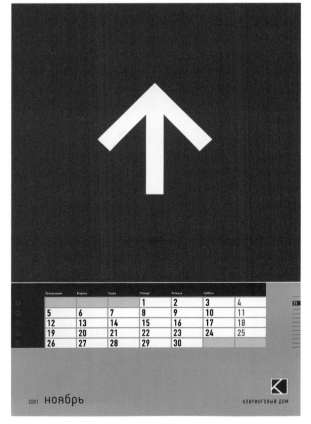

CALENDAR 2001　UKRAINE
会計会社　Financial clearing company
CL: Kliringoviy Dom　CD, D: Kuzhavsky Sergei　AD: Jitzky Stas　DF, S: OPEN！DESIGN & CONCEPTS

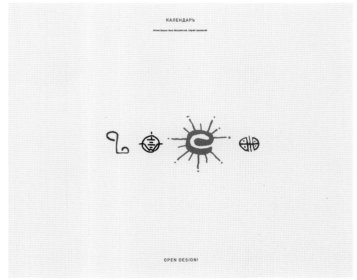

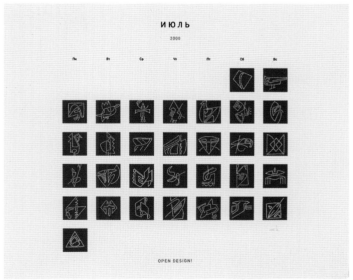

OPEN DESIGN!　2000　RUSSIA
デザイン事務所　Design firm
CL: OPEN！DESIGN & CONCEPTS　　CD, D, I: Kuzhavsky Sergei　　AD: Jitzky Stas　　I: Vse Viatskaya Anna　　DF, S: OPEN！DESIGN & CONCEPTS

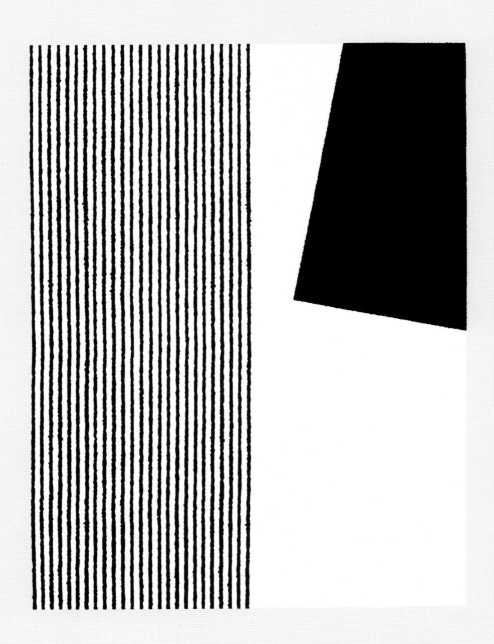

3 March

			1	2	3	**4**	5	6	7	8	9	10	**11**	12	13	14	15	16	17	**18**	19	**20**	21	22	23	24	**25**	26	27	28	29	30	31

Sun Mon Tue Wed Thu Fri Sat Sun Mon Tue Wed Thu Fri Sat Sun Mon Tue Wed Thu Fri Sat Sun Mon Tue Wed Thu Fri Sat Sun Mon Tue Wed Thu Fri Sat

1 2 3 4 5 6 7 **8** 9 10 11 12 13 14 **15** 16 17 18 19 20 21 **22** 23 24 25 26 27 28 **29** **30**

4 April

CALENDAR 2001   JAPAN
デザイン事務所 Design firm
CL: 田代卓事務所 Taku Tashiro Office   CD, AD, D: 田代　卓 Taku Tashiro   S: 田代卓事務所 Taku Tashiro Office

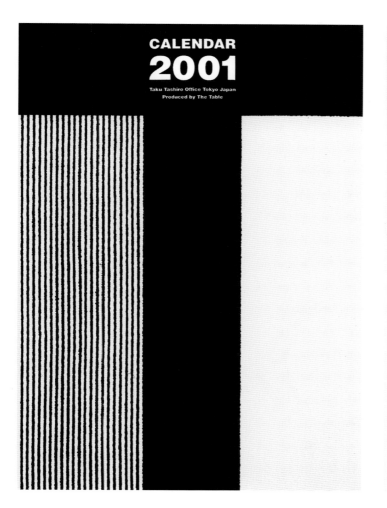

CALENDAR
2001
Taku Tashiro Office Tokyo Japan
Produced by The Table

5 May

1	2	**3**	**4**	**5**	**6**	7	8	9	10	11	12	**13**	14	15	16	17	18	19	**20**	21	22	23	24	25	26	**27**	28	29	30	31
Tue	Wed	Thu	Fri	Sat	Sun	Mon	Tue	Wed	Thu	Fri	Sat	Sun	Mon	Tue	Wed	Thu	Fri	Sat	Sun	Mon	Tue	Wed	Thu	Fri	Sat	Sun	Mon	Tue	Wed	Thu
	1	2	**3**	4	5	6	7	8	9	**10**	11	12	13	14	15	16	**17**	18	19	20	21	22	23	**24**	25	26	27	28	29	30

6 June

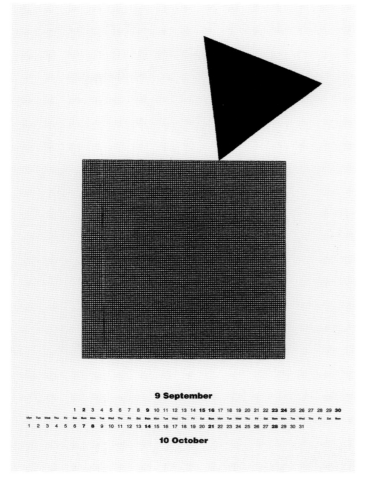

9 September

1	**2**	3	4	5	6	7	8	**9**	10	11	12	13	14	**15**	**16**	17	18	19	20	21	22	**23**	**24**	25	26	27	28	29	**30**
Mon	Tue	Wed	Thu	Fri	Sat	Sun	Mon	Tue	Wed	Thu	Fri	Sat	Sun	Mon	Tue	Wed	Thu	Fri	Sat	Sun	Mon	Tue	Wed	Thu	Fri	Sat	Sun	Mon	Tue
1	2	3	4	5	6	**7**	**8**	9	10	11	12	13	**14**	**15**	16	17	18	19	20	**21**	22	23	24	25	26	27	**28**	29	30	31

10 October

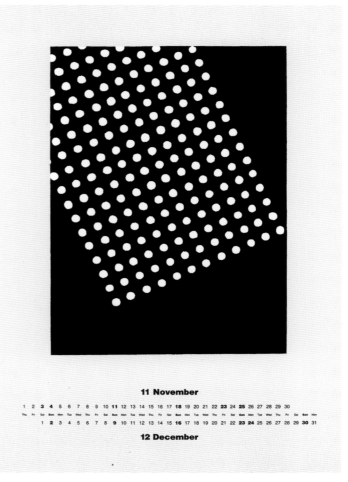

11 November

1	2	**3**	**4**	5	6	7	8	9	10	**11**	12	13	14	15	16	17	**18**	19	20	21	22	**23**	24	**25**	26	27	28	29	30
Thu	Fri	Sat	Sun	Mon	Tue	Wed	Thu	Fri	Sat	Sun	Mon	Tue	Wed	Thu	Fri	Sat	Sun	Mon	Tue	Wed	Thu	Fri	Sat	Sun	Mon	Tue	Wed	Thu	Fri
		1	**2**	3	4	5	6	7	8	**9**	10	11	12	13	14	15	**16**	17	18	19	20	21	22	**23**	**24**	25	26	27	28	29	30	**30**	31

12 December

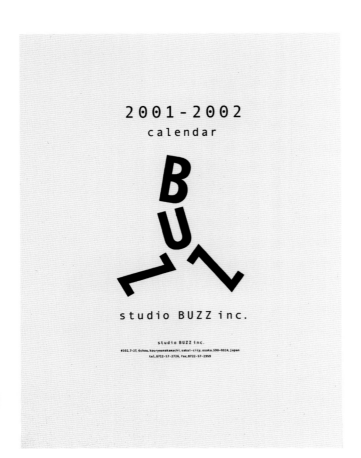

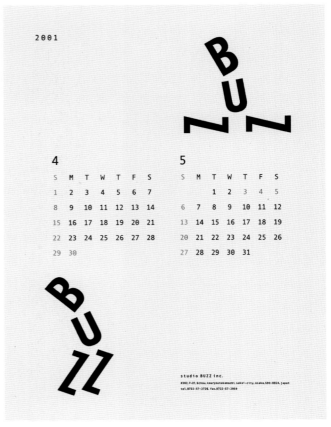

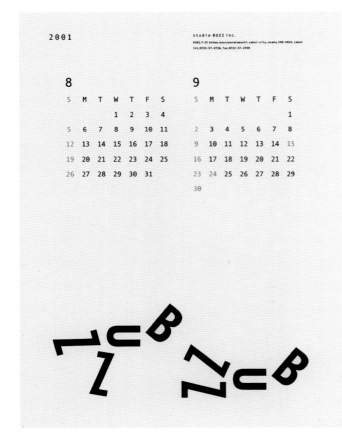

スタジオ・バズ カレンダー **Calendar for Studio BUZZ**　2002　JAPAN
プランニング会社 **Planning company**
CL: スタジオ・バズ Studio BUZZ　CD: 岸本　進 Susumu Kishimoto　AD, D: 永島　学 Manabu Nagashima　DF, S: 永島学デザイン室 Manabu Nagashima Design Inc.

PROP CALENDAR　2000　JAPAN
デザイン、印刷　Design & Printing
CL: プロップ グラフィック ステーション　PROP GRAPHIC STATION INC.　D: 矢崎由美子　Yumiko Yazaki : 松下理恵子　Rieko Matsushita　S: プロップ グラフィック ステーション　PROP GRAPHIC STATION INC.

PROP CALENDAR　1999　JAPAN
デザイン、印刷　Design & Printing
CL: プロップ グラフィック ステーション　PROP GRAPHIC STATION INC.　D: 矢崎由美子　Yumiko Yazaki : 松田恵理　Eri Matsuda　S: プロップ グラフィック ステーション　PROP GRAPHIC STATION INC.

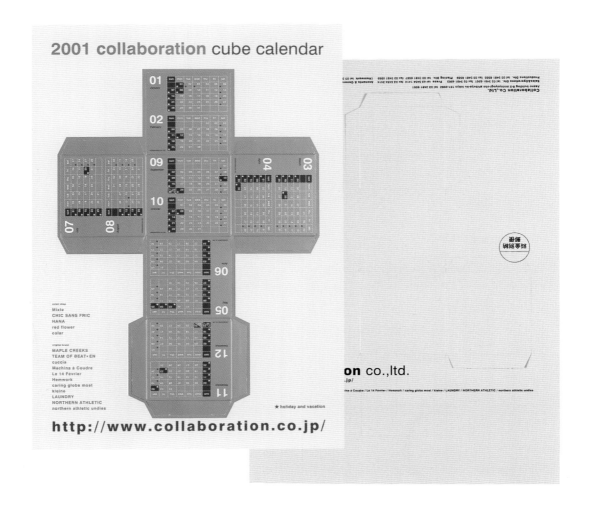

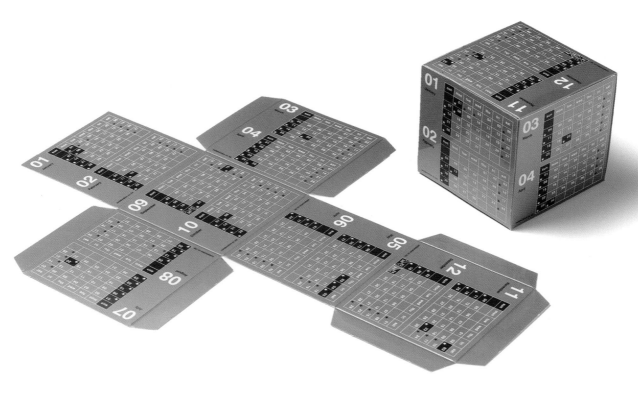

2001 コラボレーション カレンダー 2001 Collaboration Cube Calendar JAPAN

アパレル Apparel
CL: コラボレーション Collaboration co.,ltd.   AD: 青井達也／ノーザングラフィック Tatsuya Aoi / Northern Graphics   DF: ノーザングラフィック Northern Graphics   S: コラボレーション Collaboration co.,ltd.

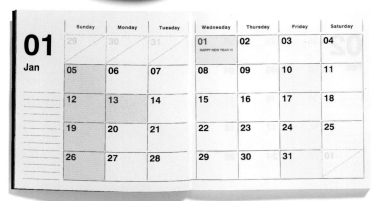

2000 コラボレーション カレンダー　2000 Collaboration Calendar　JAPAN

アパレル　Apparel

CL: コラボレーション　Collaboration co.,ltd.　Printing Director: 北川大輔／グラフ　Daisuke Kitagawa / Graph　AD: 佐藤有香／コラボレーション　Yuka Sato / Collaboration co.,ltd.
S: コラボレーション　Collaboration co.,ltd.

コラボレーション スケジュールメモ　Collaboration Schedule Memo　2003,2002　JAPAN

アパレル　Apparel

CL: コラボレーション　Collaboration co.,ltd.　AD: 青井達也／ノーザングラフィック　Tatsuya Aoi / Northern Graphics　DF: ノーザングラフィック　Northern Graphics　S: コラボレーション　Collaboration co.,ltd.

MDO 2003カレンダー　MDO 2003 CALENDAR　JAPAN
デザイン事務所　Design firm
CL: MDO　CD, AD, D: 正木　茂　Shigeru Masaki　DF, S: 正木デザイン事務所　MASAKI DESIGN OFFICE

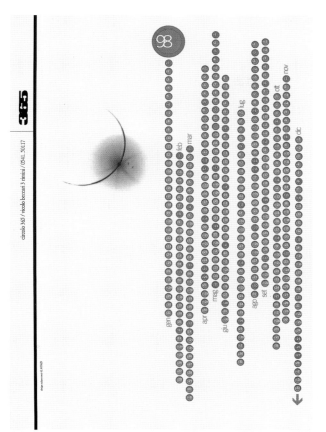

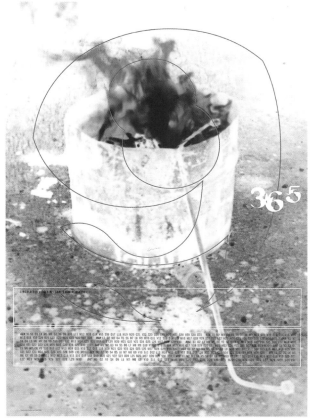

365 2000,1999,1998 ITALY
飲食業 Bar
CL: 365 MUSIC BAR　S: STEFANO TONTI DESIGN

トランス コンチネンツ・オリジナルカレンダー2003 TRANS CONTINENTS ORIGINAL CALENDAR 2003 JAPAN
アパレル Apparel
CL: ミレニアム・ジャパン MILLENNIUM JAPAN LTD.　S: ミレニアム・ジャパン MILLENNIUM JAPAN LTD.

トランス コンチネンツ・オリジナルカレンダー2002 TRANS CONTINENTS ORIGINAL CALENDAR 2002   JAPAN

アパレル Apparel
CL: ミレニアム・ジャパン MILLENNIUM JAPAN LTD.   S: ミレニアム・ジャパン MILLENNIUM JAPAN LTD.

2003 CALENDAR   JAPAN

イラストレーション制作 Illustration studio
CL: 山本イラストレーション制作室 Yamamoto Illustration Studio   CD, AD, I: 山本重也 Shigeya Yamamoto   S: 山本イラストレーション制作室 Yamamoto Illustration Studio

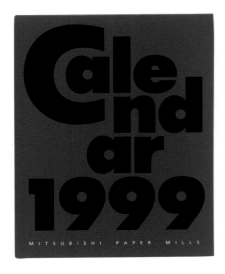

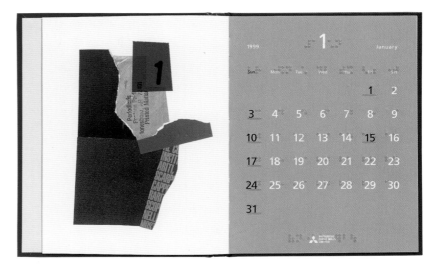

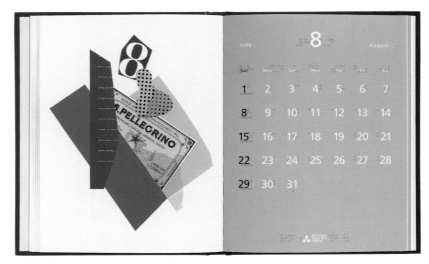

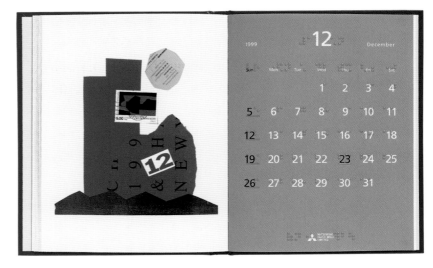

三菱 点字カレンダー1999　MITSUBISHI BRAILLE CALENDAR 1999　　JAPAN

製紙　Paper manufacturer
CL: 三菱製紙　MITSUBISHI PAPER MILLS LIMITED　　AD: 小島良平　Ryohei Kojima　　D: 神戸　睦　Atsushi Kanbe　　DF, S: 小島良平デザイン事務所　RYOHEI KOJIMA DESIGN OFFICE

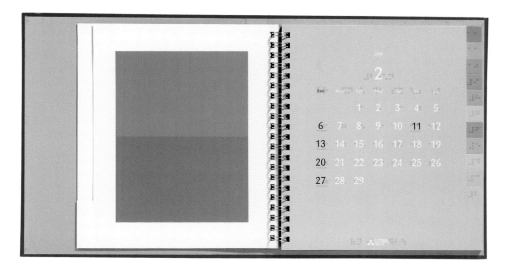

2000 BRAILLE CALENDAR　JAPAN

製紙　Paper manufacturer
CL: 三菱製紙　MITSUBISHI PAPER MILLS LIMITED　　AD: 小島良平　Ryohei Kojima　　D: 北島　栄　Sakae Kitajima　　DF, S: 小島良平デザイン事務所　RYOHEI KOJIMA DESIGN OFFICE

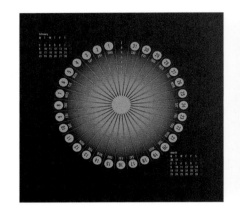  

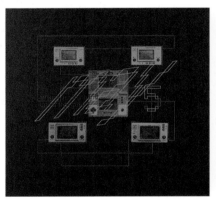  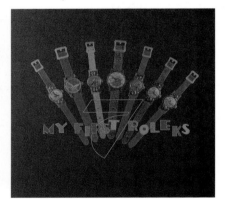

MEMORIES　1998　SINGAPORE
印刷、製紙業　Printer & Paper merchant
CL: PRINT DYNAMICS & SHRIRO PAPER　CD, AD, D: Hon Soo Tien　P: Charlie Lim Photography　DF, S: HON'S DESIGN

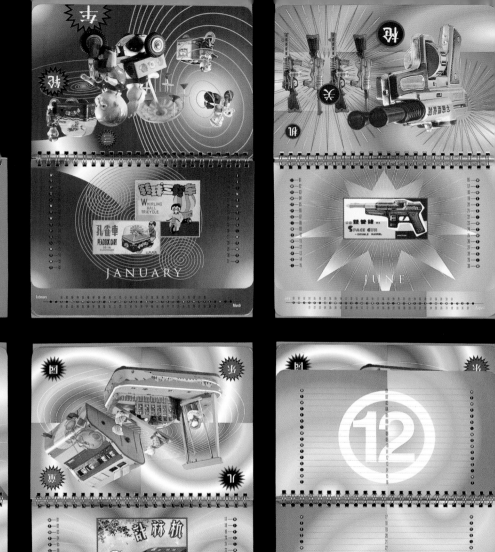

2003 August 08

sunday	monday	tuesday	wednesday	thursday	friday	saturday
7/27	7/28	7/29	7/30	7/31	1	2
3	4	5	6	7	8	9
10	11	12	13	14	15	16
17	18	19	20	21	22	23
24/31	25	26	27	28	29	30

2003 September 09

sunday	monday	tuesday	wednesday	thursday	friday	saturday
8/31	1	2	3	4	5	6
7	8	9	10	11	12	13
14	15 Respect for the Aged Day	16	17	18	19	20
21	22	23 Autumnal Equinox Day	24	25	26	27
28	29	30	10/1	10/2	10/3	10/4

03

2003 January 01

sunday	monday	tuesday	wednesday	thursday	friday	saturday
	2002 12/30	2002 12/31	1 New Year's Day	2	3	4
5	6	7	8	9	10	11
12	13 Coming of Age Day	14	15	16	17	18
19	20	21	22	23	24	25
26	27	28	29	30	31	2/1

2003 April 04

sunday	monday	tuesday	wednesday	thursday	friday	saturday
3/30	3/31	1	2	3	4	5
6	7	8	9	10	11	12
13	14	15	16	17	18	19
20	21	22	23	24	25	26
27	28	29 National Day	30	5/1	5/2	5/3 Constitution Day

2003 CALENDAR　JAPAN

総合的な広告宣伝計画の立案　Advertisement planning
CL: butterfly·stroke inc. / John and Jane Doe Inc.　　CD, AD: 青木克憲　Katsunori Aoki　　Artist: 村上　隆　Takashi Murakami　　DF: butterfly·stroke inc. / John and Jane Doe Inc.　　S: butterfly·stroke inc.

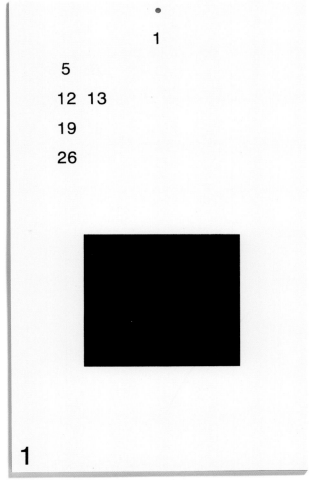

HOLIDAY ホリデイ　2003 JAPAN
メーカー、広告制作 Maker & Advertising
CL: D-BROS　CD: 宮田　識　Satoru Miyata　AD, D, I: 柿木原政広　Masahiro Kakinokihara　Producer: 中岡美奈子　Minako Nakaoka　DF: ドラフト　DRAFT co.,ltd.　S: D-BROS

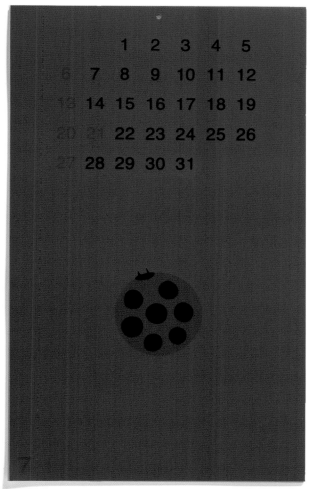

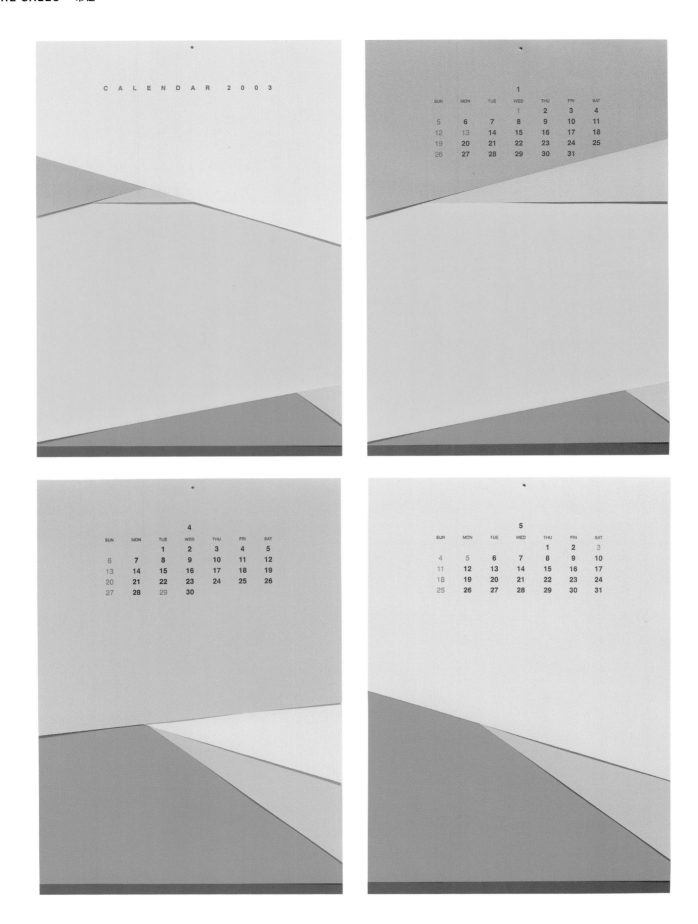

CALENDAR 2003　　JAPAN
グラフィックデザイン、出版　Graphic design & Publication
CL: ワンストローク　ONE STROKE　　AD, D: 駒形克己　Katsumi Komagata　　DF, S: ワンストローク　ONE STROKE

ROLL UP CALENDAR　2003　JAPAN

グラフィックデザイン、出版　**Graphic design & Publication**
CL: ワンストローク　ONE STROKE　　AD, D, I: 駒形克己　Katsumi Komagata　　DF, S: ワンストローク　ONE STROKE

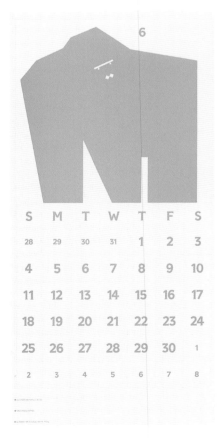

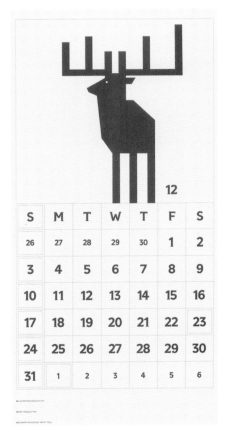

ANIMAL SCRAPTURE　アニマル スクラプチャー　2000　JAPAN
製紙　Paper manufacturer
CL: 王子製紙　OJI PAPER　CD, AD, I: 伊藤勝一　Katsuichi Ito　D: 藤原俊哉　Toshiya Fujiwara　DF, S: 伊藤勝一デザイン室　KATSUICHI ITO DESIGN OFFICE

1997
CALENDAR
SCRAPTURE :
USI

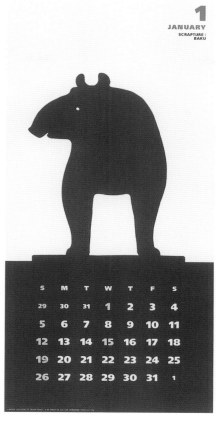

1
JANUARY
SCRAPTURE :
BAKU

S	M	T	W	T	F	S
29	30	31	1	2	3	4
5	6	7	8	9	10	11
12	13	14	15	16	17	18
19	20	21	22	23	24	25
26	27	28	29	30	31	1

4
APRIL
SCRAPTURE :
MUSASABI

S	M	T	W	T	F	S
30	31	1	2	3	4	5
6	7	8	9	10	11	12
13	14	15	16	17	18	19
20	21	22	23	24	25	26
27	28	29	30	1	2	3

6
JUNE
SCRAPTURE :
MANDRILL

S	M	T	W	T	F	S
1	2	3	4	5	6	7
8	9	10	11	12	13	14
15	16	17	18	19	20	21
22	23	24	25	26	27	28
29	30	1	2	3	4	5

9
SEPTEMBER
SCRAPTURE :
AHODORI

S	M	T	W	T	F	S
31	1	2	3	4	5	6
7	8	9	10	11	12	13
14	15	16	17	18	19	20
21	22	23	24	25	26	27
28	29	30	1	2	3	4

12
DECEMBER
SCRAPTURE :
IMPALA

S	M	T	W	T	F	S
30	1	2	3	4	5	6
7	8	9	10	11	12	13
14	15	16	17	18	19	20
21	22	23	24	25	26	27
28	29	30	31	1	2	3

ANIMAL SCRAPTURE　アニマル スクラプチャー　1997　JAPAN
製紙　Paper manufacturer
CL: 王子製紙　OJI PAPER　CD, AD, I: 伊藤勝一　Katsuichi Ito　D: 藤原俊哉　Toshiya Fujiwara　DF, S: 伊藤勝一デザイン室　KATSUICHI ITO DESIGN OFFICE

1

S	M	T	W	T	F	S
			1	2	3	4	5
6	7	8	9	10	11	12
13	14	15	16	17	18	19
20	21	22	23	24	25	26
27	28	29	30	31		

2

S	M	T	W	T	F	S
					1	2
3	4	5	6	7	8	9
10	11	12	13	14	15	16
17	18	19	20	21	22	23
24	25	26	27	28		

TETSURO OKABE CALENDAR 2002

8

S	M	T	W	T	F	S
				1	2	3
4	5	6	7	8	9	10
11	12	13	14	15	16	17
18	19	20	21	22	23	24
25	26	27	28	29	30	31

9

S	M	T	W	T	F	S
1	2	3	4	5	6	7
8	9	10	11	12	13	14
15	16	17	18	19	20	21
22	23	24	25	26	27	28
29	30					

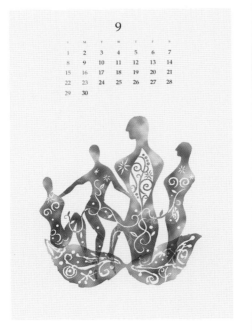

スパイラルカレンダー　Spiral Calendar 2002 JAPAN
アート商品・雑貨の販売　Sales of art product & miscellaneous goods
CL: スパイラル　Spiral　AD, S: 岡部哲郎　Tetsuro Okabe

スパイラルカレンダー　Spiral Calendar　2003,2002　JAPAN
アート商品・雑貨の販売　Sales of art product & miscellaneous goods
CL: スパイラル　Spiral　AD, S: 岡部哲郎　Tetsuro Okabe

CALENDAR 2000　JAPAN
グラフィックデザイン、出版　Graphic design & Publication
CL: ワンストローク　ONE STROKE　AD, D, I: 駒形克己　Katsumi Komagata　DF, S: ワンストローク　ONE STROKE

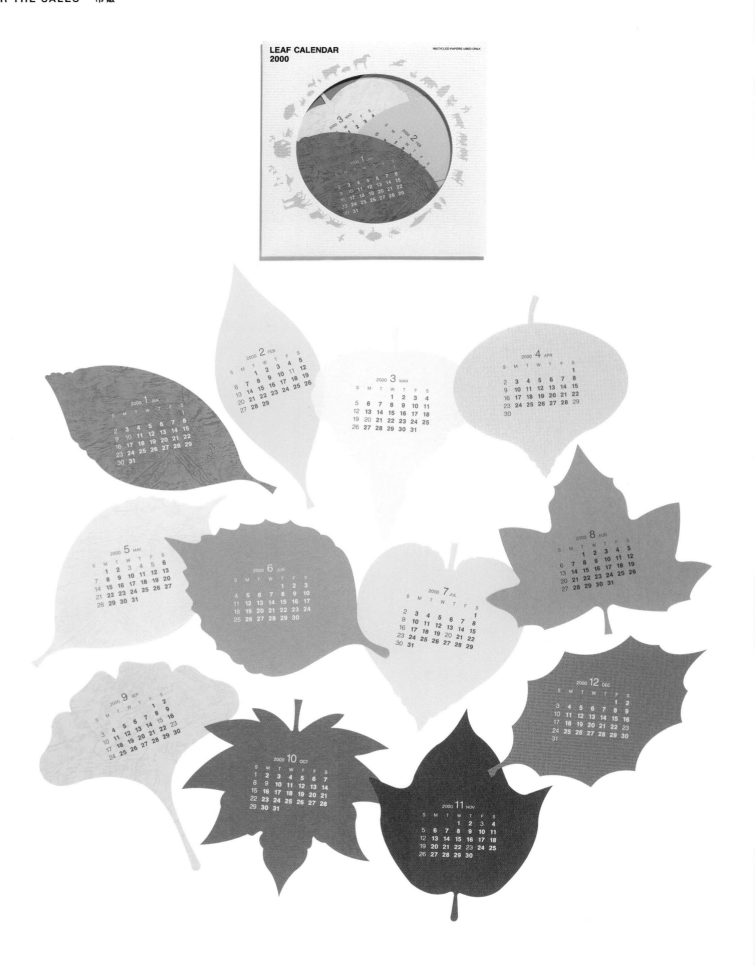

LEAF CALENDAR 2000　JAPAN
グラフィックデザイン、出版　Graphic design & Publication
CL: ワンストローク　ONE STROKE　AD, D, I: 駒形克己　Katsumi Komagata　DF, S: ワンストローク　ONE STROKE

広告・SP・パッケージの企画・制作　AD, SP, Package-design

Leaf Calendar　1997　JAPAN
広告・SP・パッケージの企画・制作　AD, SP, Package-design
CL: 第一紙行　DAIICHISHIKO CO.,LTD.　CD, AD, D, S: 徳永裕二　Yuji Tokunaga　DF: 第一紙行　DAIICHISHIKO CO.,LTD.

卓上・壁掛カレンダー 空　Desk Calendar "SKY"　2003　JAPAN
ステーショナリーの製造　Stationery manufacturer
CL: ジー・シー　G・C inc.　S: ジー・シー　G・C inc.

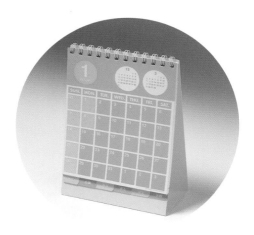

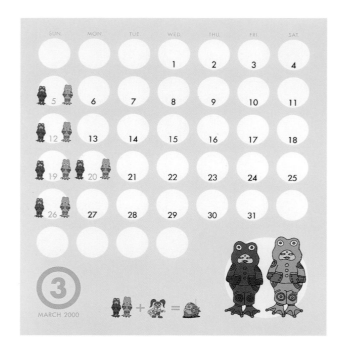

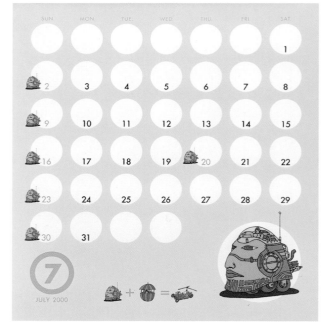

Stand・pop Typo　スタンド・ポップタイポ　2001　JAPAN
広告・SP・パッケージの企画・制作　AD, SP, Package-design
CL: 第一紙行　DAIICHISHIKO CO.,LTD.　CD, AD, D, I, S: 徳永裕二　Yuji Tokunaga　DF: 第一紙行　DAIICHISHIKO CO.,LTD.

THE WONDER CHARACTERS CALENDAR　ザ・ワンダーキャラクターズ カレンダー　2000　JAPAN
広告・SP・パッケージの企画・制作　AD, SP, Package-design
CL: 第一紙行　DAIICHISHIKO CO.,LTD.　CD, AD, D, I, S: 徳永裕二　Yuji Tokunaga　DF: 第一紙行　DAIICHISHIKO CO.,LTD.

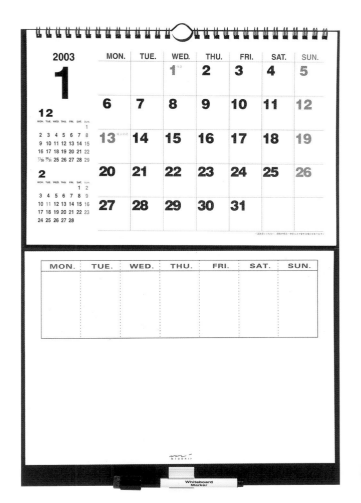

ホワイトボードカレンダー Whiteboard Calendar 2003 JAPAN

紙製品及び文房具の製造・販売 Manufacture & sales of paper products & stationery
CL: ミドリ MIDORI CO.,LTD.   S: ミドリ企画部 MIDORI CO.,LTD. / Planning Dept.

卓上2マンス カレンダー Desk Calendar "Two Months" 2003 JAPAN

カレンダーの製造・販売 Calendar supplier
CL: エヌ・プランニング N・PLANNING CO.,LTD.   CD: 板垣雅文 Masafumi Itagaki   S: エヌ・プランニング N・PLANNING CO.,LTD.

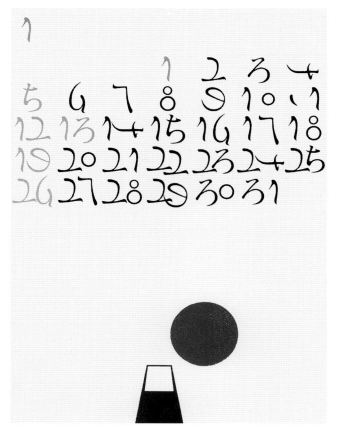

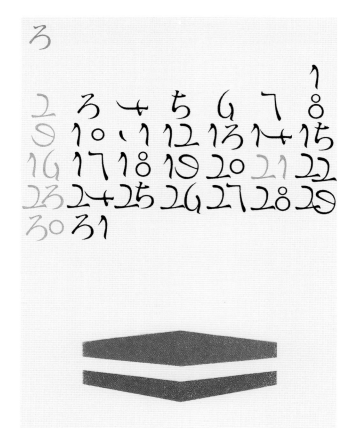

I·RO·HA　いろは　2003　JAPAN

メーカー、広告制作　Maker & Advertising
CL: D-BROS　CD: 宮田　識　Satoru Miyata　AD, D, I: 田中竜介　Ryusuke Tanaka　Producer: 中岡美奈子　Minako Nakaoka　DF: ドラフト　DRAFT co.,ltd.　S: D-BROS

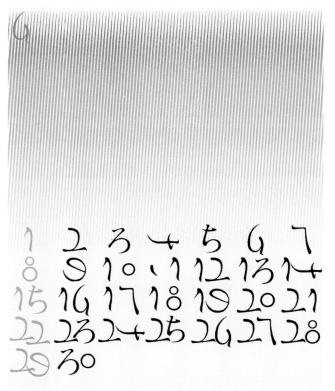

祥洲 ジュウニコノ月 Twelve MOONS   2002 JAPAN
広告・SP・パッケージの企画・制作 AD, SP, Package-design
CL: 第一紙行 DAIICHISHIKO CO.,LTD.   CD, AD, D, S: 徳永裕二 Yuji Tokunaga   CW, Calligrapher: 祥洲 Shosyu   DF: 第一紙行 DAIICHISHIKO CO.,LTD.

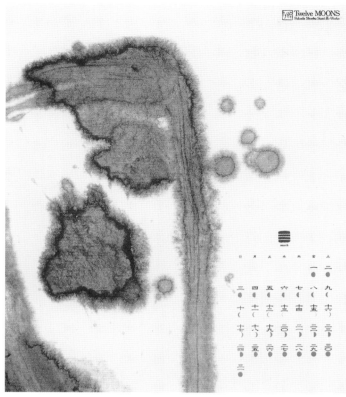

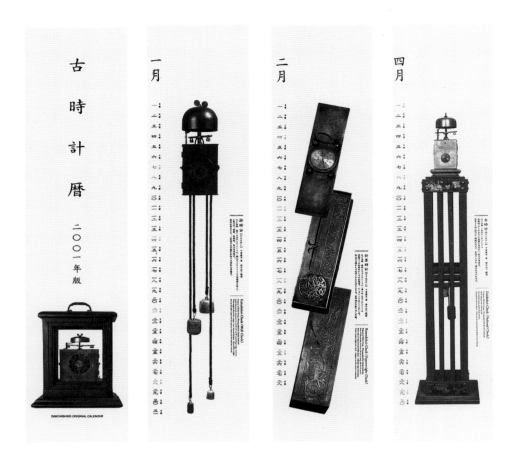

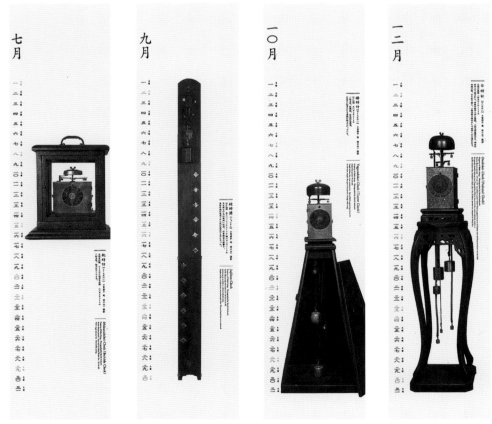

古時計暦　Old Clock Calendar　2001　JAPAN

広告・SP・パッケージの企画・制作　AD, SP, Package-design
CL: 第一紙行　DAIICHISHIKO CO.,LTD.　CD, AD, D, S: 梶めぐみ　Megumi Kaji　P: 猪口公一　Koichi Inoguchi　CW: 正井彩香　Ayaka Masai　DF: 第一紙行　DAIICHISHIKO CO.,LTD.

※千賀耕平氏のコレクションを掲載。参考文献：（株）マリア書房発行　骨董「緑青」Vol.2 特集 古時計
　From the Senga Kohei Collection. Reference: Kottou "Rokusho" (Antique "Patina") Vol. 2 Special edition "Furudokei (Antique clocks)" published by MARIA SHOBO Co.,Ltd.

あかり暦 Light Calendar 2002 JAPAN

広告・SP・パッケージの企画・制作 AD, SP, Package-design
CL: 第一紙行 DAIICHISHIKO CO.,LTD. CD, AD, D, S: 梶めぐみ Megumi Kaji P: 猪口公一 Koichi Inoguchi Supervisor, Text: 坪内富士夫 Fujio Tsubouchi DF: 第一紙行 DAIICHISHIKO CO.,LTD.

※教證寺住職坪内富士夫氏のコレクションを掲載。参考文献：(株)マリア書房発行 骨董「緑青」Vol.1 特集 あかり
From the collection of Kyoshoji Temple head priest Tsubouchi Fujio.Reference: Kottou "Rokusho" (Antique "Patina") Vol. 1 "Akari (Light)" published by MARIA SHOBO Co.,Ltd.

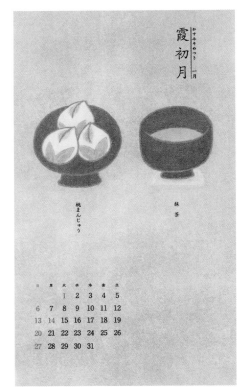

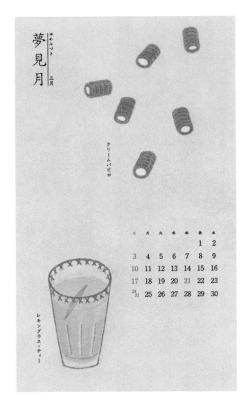

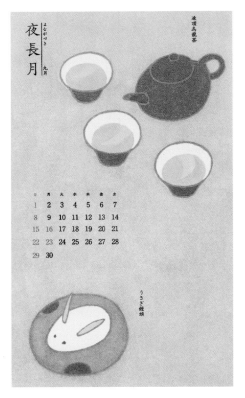

喫茶暦　KISSA-GOYOMI　2002　JAPAN

広告・SP・パッケージの企画・制作　AD, SP, Package-design
CL: 第一紙行　DAIICHISHIKO CO.,LTD.　CD, CW, S: 正井彩香　Ayaka Masai　AD, D: 雨森千尋　Chihiro Amenomori　I: 成富小百合　Sayuri Naritomi　DF: 第一紙行　DAIICHISHIKO CO.,LTD.

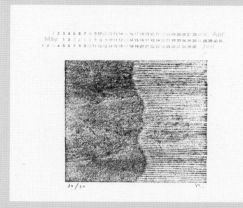

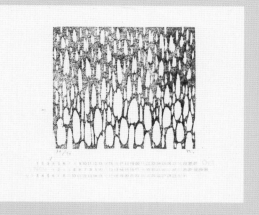

ICL松永かのオリジナルカレンダー2002　ICL Kano Matsunaga Original Calendar 2002　JAPAN
ファッション・雑貨の企画販売と飲食店の経営　Planning & Sales of fashion, miscellaneous goods. Management of restaurants
CL: SAZABY Inc.　CD, AD, I: 松永かの　Kano Matsunaga　S: SAZABY Inc.

デスクトップカレンダー　DESK TOP CALENDAR　2003 JAPAN
グラフィックデザイン及びプロダクトのデザイン・製造・販売　Graphic design & Design, Manufacture, Sales of product
CL: カクラ　KAKURA　CD, AD, D: 石原ゆかり　Yukari Ishihara　S: カクラ　KAKURA

2002年版 古器と野の花こよみ　Antiques and Flowers of the Field Calendar 2002　JAPAN

広告・SP・パッケージの企画・制作　AD, SP, Package-design
CL: 第一紙行　DAIICHISHIKO CO.,LTD.　CD, AD, D, S: 梶めぐみ　Megumi Kaji　P: 藤井友樹　Tomoki Fujii　Flower Arrangement: 守田　蔵　Kura Morita　DF: 第一紙行　DAIICHISHIKO CO.,LTD.

※(株)マリア書房より発行の別冊「緑青」に掲載された写真・注釈・略歴等を、許可を得て使用・構成
　Photographs, notes, profile, &c. published by MARIA SHOBO Co.,Ltd. in the special edition "Rokusho (Patina)" and used with their permission

七月
文月（ふみづき）／ July

黄瀬戸片口
Yellow Seto ware beaked bowl
高　十一・五センチメートル
口径　十八×十五・四センチメートル
花　ひつじ草

十月
神無月（かんなづき）／ October

根来足付角切盆
Negoro lacquer tray with four feet
高　七・二センチメートル
径　三十六・七センチメートル
花　榠樝

十二月
師走（しわす）／ December

時代鉄釣灯火燭
Iron hanging oil lamp
高　二十五センチメートル
軸　三十二・五センチメートル
唐津小服茶碗
Karatsu ware tea bowl
高　五・八センチメートル
口径　十センチメートル
花　山茶花

七月

日	月	火	水	木	金	土
	先勝 一	友引 二	先負 三	仏滅 四	大安 五	赤口 六
先勝 七	友引 八	先負 九	仏滅 十	大安 十一	赤口 十二	先勝 十三
友引 十四	先負 十五	仏滅 十六	大安 十七	赤口 十八	先勝 十九	友引 二十
先負 二十一	仏滅 二十二	大安 二十三	赤口 二十四	先勝 二十五	友引 二十六	先負 二十七
仏滅 二十八	大安 二十九	赤口 三十	先勝 三十一			

十月

日	月	火	水	木	金	土
		先勝 一	友引 二	先負 三	仏滅 四	大安 五
赤口 六	先勝 七	友引 八	先負 九	仏滅 十	大安 十一	赤口 十二
先勝 十三	友引 十四	先負 十五	仏滅 十六	大安 十七	赤口 十八	先勝 十九
友引 二十	先負 二十一	仏滅 二十二	大安 二十三	赤口 二十四	先勝 二十五	友引 二十六
先負 二十七	仏滅 二十八	大安 二十九	赤口 三十	先勝 三十一		

十二月

日	月	火	水	木	金	土
赤口 一	先勝 二	友引 三	先負 四	仏滅 五	大安 六	赤口 七
先勝 八	友引 九	先負 十	仏滅 十一	大安 十二	赤口 十三	先勝 十四
友引 十五	先負 十六	仏滅 十七	大安 十八	赤口 十九	先勝 二十	友引 二十一
先負 二十二	仏滅 二十三	大安 二十四	赤口 二十五	先勝 二十六	友引 二十七	先負 二十八
仏滅 二十九	大安 三十	赤口 三十一				

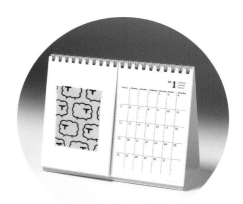

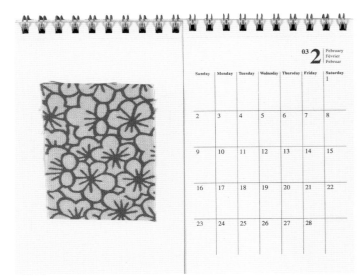

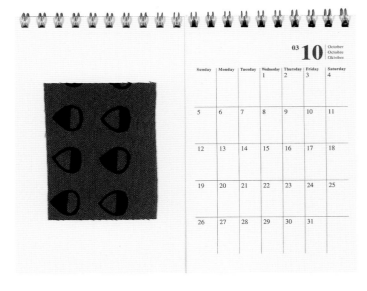

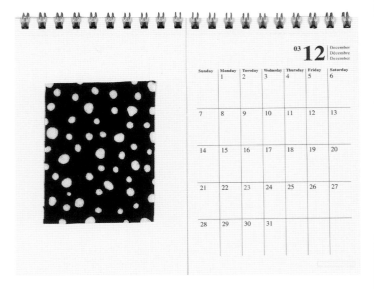

てぬぐいカレンダー　TENUGUI CALENDAR　2003　JAPAN
複合セレクトショップ　Fashion cross merchandising store
CL: イッツ デモ　ITS' DEMO　S: イッツ デモ　ITS' DEMO

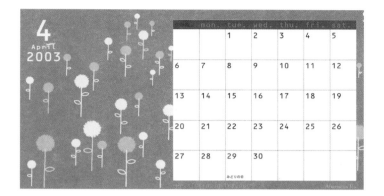

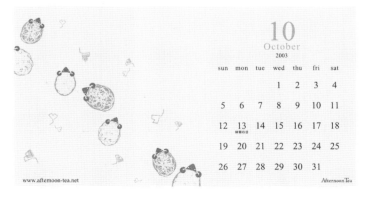

アフタヌーンティーリビング　バードカレンダー卓上2003 Afternoon Tea Living BIRD Calendar 2003　JAPAN
ファッション・雑貨の企画販売と飲食店の経営　Planning & Sales of fashion, miscellaneous goods. Management of restaurants
CL: SAZABY Inc.　CD: 松倉一美　Hitomi Matsukura　D: 山崎美幸　Miyuki Yamazaki　S: SAZABY Inc.

アフタヌーンティーリビング　シープカレンダー卓上2003 Afternoon Tea Living SHEEP Calendar 2003　JAPAN
ファッション・雑貨の企画販売と飲食店の経営　Planning & Sales of fashion, miscellaneous goods. Management of restaurants
CL: SAZABY Inc.　CD: 松倉一美　Hitomi Matsukura　D: 山崎美幸　Miyuki Yamazaki　S: SAZABY Inc.

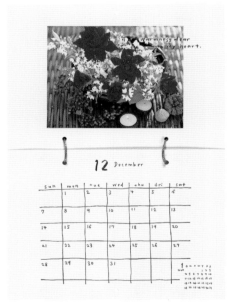

Asian Flower Calendar　2003　JAPAN

紙製品及び雑貨の企画・制作・販売　Production of paper products & miscellaneous goods
CL: リュリュ　Ryu-Ryu Co.,Ltd.　CD: 西巻　眞　Makoto Nishimaki　D: 稲生綾子　Ayako Inou　P: 奥村康人　Yasuto Okumura　DF, S: リュリュ　Ryu-Ryu Co.,Ltd.

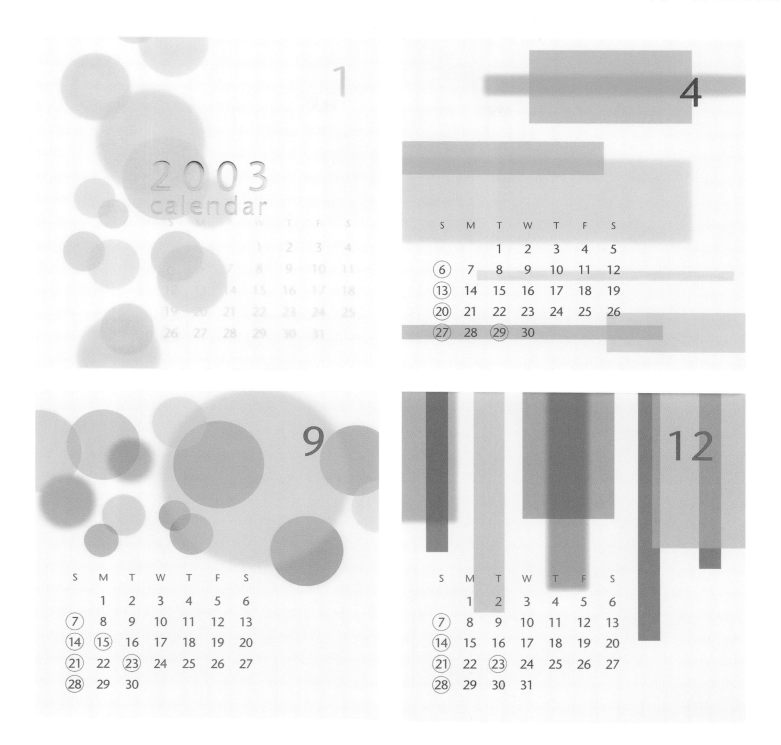

1

2003
calendar

S	M	T	W	T	F	S
			1	2	3	4
5	6	7	8	9	10	11
12	13	14	15	16	17	18
19	20	21	22	23	24	25
26	27	28	29	30	31	

4

S	M	T	W	T	F	S
		1	2	3	4	5
(6)	7	8	9	10	11	12
(13)	14	15	16	17	18	19
(20)	21	22	23	24	25	26
(27)	28	(29)	30			

9

S	M	T	W	T	F	S
	1	2	3	4	5	6
(7)	8	9	10	11	12	13
(14)	(15)	16	17	18	19	20
(21)	22	(23)	24	25	26	27
(28)	29	30				

12

S	M	T	W	T	F	S
	1	2	3	4	5	6
(7)	8	9	10	11	12	13
(14)	15	16	17	18	19	20
(21)	22	(23)	24	25	26	27
(28)	29	30	31			

フロスト　FROST　2003　JAPAN

ギフトラッピング及びファッショングッズの企画販売　Manufacture & whole saler for gift wrapping products
CL: ゾナルトアンドカンパニー　ZONART & CO.,LTD.　CD: 木村　勝　Katsu Kimura　AD: 中島千鶴　Chizuru Nakajima　D: 中村あい　Ai Nakamura
DF: パッケージングディレクション　Katsu Kimura & Packaging Direction CO.,LTD.　S: ゾナルトアンドカンパニー　ZONART & CO.,LTD.

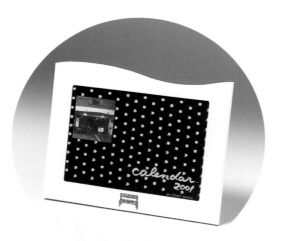

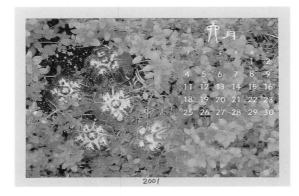

ブルパンキーノ 2001 オリジナルカレンダー　Blu Panchino 2001 Original Calendar　JAPAN
アンティークショップ　Antique shop
CL: ブルパンキーノ　Blu Panchino　S: ブルパンキーノ　Blu Panchino

2 Feb.

S	M	T	W	T	F	S
						1
2	3	4	5	6	7	8
9	10	11	12	13	14	15
16	17	18	19	20	21	22
23	24	25	26	27	28	

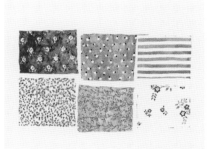

4 Apr.

S	M	T	W	T	F	S
		1	2	3	4	5
6	7	8	9	10	11	12
13	14	15	16	17	18	19
20	21	22	23	24	25	26
27	28	29	30			

5 May

S	M	T	W	T	F	S
				1	2	3
4	5	6	7	8	9	10
11	12	13	14	15	16	17
18	19	20	21	22	23	24
25	26	27	28	29	30	31

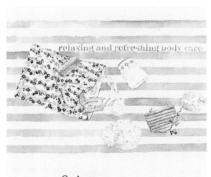

8 Aug.

S	M	T	W	T	F	S
					1	2
3	4	5	6	7	8	9
10	11	12	13	14	15	16
17	18	19	20	21	22	23
24	25	26	27	28	29	30
31						

10 Oct.

S	M	T	W	T	F	S
			1	2	3	4
5	6	7	8	9	10	11
12	13	14	15	16	17	18
19	20	21	22	23	24	25
26	27	28	29	30	31	

12 Dec.

S	M	T	W	T	F	S
	1	2	3	4	5	6
7	8	9	10	11	12	13
14	15	16	17	18	19	20
21	22	23	24	25	26	27
28	29	30	31			

アフタヌーンティーリビング　水彩カレンダー卓上2003　Afternoon Tea Living Water-Color Calendar 2003　JAPAN
ファッション・雑貨の企画販売と飲食店の経営　Planning & Sales of fashion, miscellaneous goods. Management of restaurants
CL: SAZABY Inc.　CD: 松倉一美　Hitomi Matsukura　D: 山崎美幸　Miyuki Yamazaki　I: 福本麻里　Mari Fukumoto　S: SAZABY Inc.

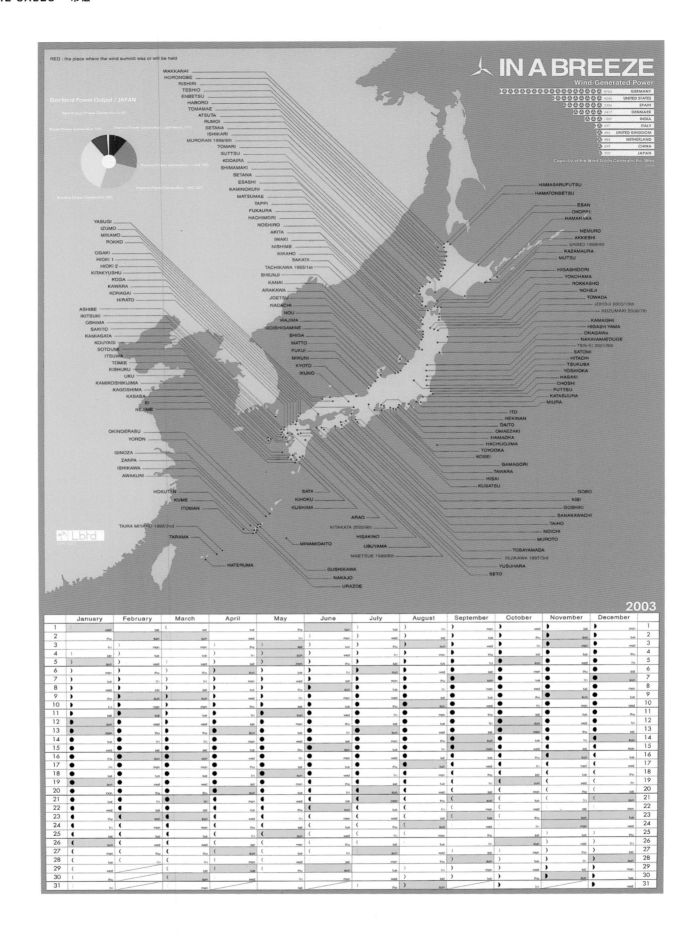

IN A BREEZE 風力発電所マップ 2003 JAPAN

デザイン及びプロダクト制作 Design & Product production
CL: 野方電機工業 デザインプロダクト部 Nogata Denki Kogyo Co.,Ltd.　CD, D: 狩野潤哉 Junya Kano　S: Creative Resource Institute Inc.

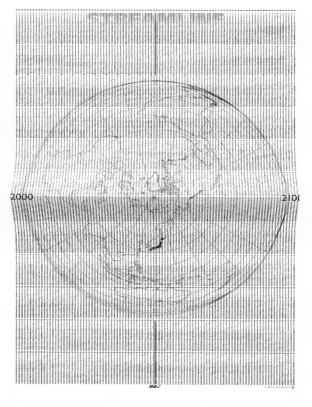

STREAMLINE　2000　JAPAN

空輸業　Airlines

CL: 全日空商事　All Nippon Airways　　CD: 中村克彦　Katsuhiko Nakamura　　AD, D: 杉崎真之助　Shinnoske Sugisaki　　P: 小沢治彦　Luke H.Ozawa　　DF, S: 真之助事務所　Shinnoske Inc.

12枚組のカレンダーと、地図上に2000年から3000年までの日付を記載したポスターカレンダーのセット　　A 12-page calendar plus poster calendar, showing dates from 2000 to 3000 on a map, set.

2003年版 週めくり 東京美女カレンダー　2003 Tokyo Beauty Calendar　JAPAN
ステーショナリーの製造　Stationery manufacturer
CL: ピンナップ　PIN UP CO.,LTD.　CD: 中村眞一　Shinichi Nakamura　D: 平野貴子　Takako Hirano　P: 風丸　KAZEMARU　S: ピンナップ　PIN UP CO.,LTD.

OYAJI CALENDAR 2002　おやじカレンダー 2002　JAPAN

芸能プロダクション　Public entertainments production
CL: プランチャイム　Plan Chime　AD, D, CW: 吉野修平　Shuhei Yoshino　P: 橘　蓮二　Renji Tachibana　DF, S: ヨシノデザインオフィス　Yoshino Design Office Inc.

Free Soul Man　2002　JAPAN

美術館　Museum
CL: 原美術館　Hara Museum of Contemporary Art　CD: 青野和子　Kazuko Aono　AD, D: 梶谷芳郎　Yoshiro Kajitani　D: 大杉晋也　Shinya Osugi　P: 三橋　純　Jun Mitsuhashi　DF, S: 梶谷デザイン　KAJITANY

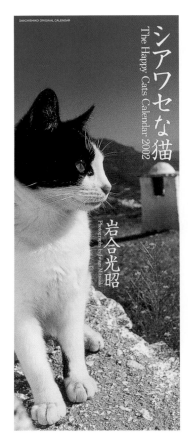

岩合光昭 シアワセな猫　The Happy Cats Calendar　2002　JAPAN
広告・SP・パッケージの企画・制作　AD, SP, Package-design
CL: 第一紙行　DAIICHISHIKO CO.,LTD.　CD, AD, D, S: 徳永裕二　Yuji Tokunaga　P, CW: 岩合光昭　Mitsuaki Iwago　DF: 第一紙行　DAIICHISHIKO CO.,LTD.

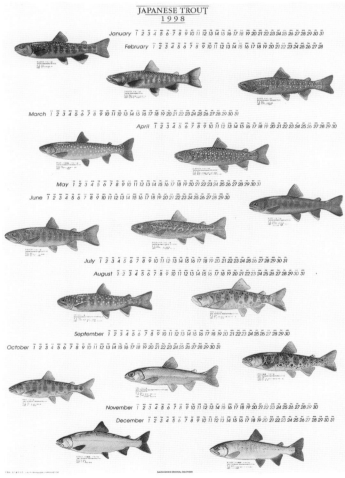

ペンギンズ　アイランド　PENGUINS ISLAND　1999　JAPAN
広告・SP・パッケージの企画・制作　AD, SP, Package-design
CL: 第一紙行　DAIICHISHIKC CO.,LTD.　CD, AD, D, S: 橋本　隆　Takashi Hashimoto　Artist: 藤井厚志　Atsushi Fujii　DF: 第一紙行　DAIICHISHIKO CO.,LTD.

ジャパニーズ　トラウト　JAPANESE TROUT　1998　JAPAN
広告・SP・パッケージの企画・制作　AD, SP, Package-design
CL: 第一紙行　DAIICHISHIKC CO.,LTD.　CD, AD, D, S: 橋本　隆　Takashi Hashimoto　Artist: 藤井厚志　Atsushi Fujii　DF: 第一紙行　DAIICHISHIKO CO.,LTD.

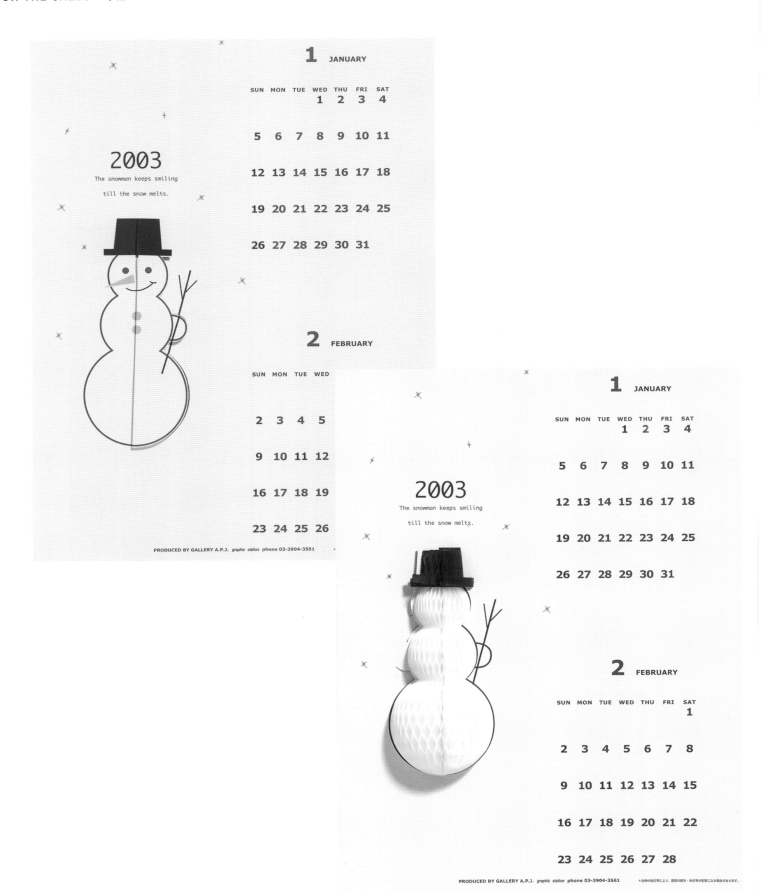

ハニカムカレンダー 2003 Honey Comb Calendar 2003　JAPAN
ステーショナリーと雑貨の企画・デザイン・製造 Production of stationery & miscellaneous goods
CL: アートプリントジャパン ART PRINT JAPAN CO.,LTD.　CD, AD, D, I: スタウト 淑子 Toshiko Stout　CW: Michael Stout　S: アートプリントジャパン ART PRINT JAPAN CO.,LTD.

5 MAY

SUN	MON	TUE	WED	THU	FRI	SAT
				1	2	3
4	5	6	7	8	9	10
11	12	13	14	15	16	17
18	19	20	21	22	23	24
25	26	27	28	29	30	31

2003
Gray skies now above.
Bobbing umbrellas below
colour triumphs.

6 JUNE

SUN	MON	TUE	WED	THU	FRI	SAT
1	2	3	4	5	6	7
8	9	10	11	12	13	14
15	16	17	18	19	20	21
22	23	24	25	26	27	28
29	30					

PRODUCED BY GALLERY A.P.J. graphic station phone 03-3904-3561

7 JULY

SUN	MON	TUE	WED	THU	FRI	SAT
		1	2	3	4	5
6	7	8	9	10	11	12
13	14	15	16	17	18	19
20	21	22	23	24	25	26
27	28	29	30	31		

2003
Gray brick wall
Giant sunflowers grow tall
even in cities.

8 AUGUST

SUN	MON	TUE	WED	THU	FRI	SAT
					1	2
3	4	5	6	7	8	9
10	11	12	13	14	15	16
17	18	19	20	21	22	23
24	25	26	27	28	29	30
31						

PRODUCED BY GALLERY A.P.J. graphic station phone 03-3904-3561

9 SEPTEMBER

SUN	MON	TUE	WED	THU	FRI	SAT
	1	2	3	4	5	6
7	8	9	10	11	12	13
14	15	16	17	18	19	20
21	22	23	24	25	26	27
28	29	30				

2003
Fresh fallen leaves lie
under feet in search of sweets
a trick or a treat.

10 OCTOBER

SUN	MON	TUE	WED	THU	FRI	SAT
			1	2	3	4
5	6	7	8	9	10	11
12	13	14	15	16	17	18
19	20	21	22	23	24	25
26	27	28	29	30	31	

PRODUCED BY GALLERY A.P.J. graphic station phone 03-3904-3561

11 NOVEMBER

SUN	MON	TUE	WED	THU	FRI	SAT
						1
2	3	4	5	6	7	8
9	10	11	12	13	14	15
16	17	18	19	20	21	22
23	24	25	26	27	28	29
30						

2003
Pine gum scent in the air
Roasted chestnuts and holly
red and white ribbons.

12 DECEMBER

SUN	MON	TUE	WED	THU	FRI	SAT
	1	2	3	4	5	6
7	8	9	10	11	12	13
14	15	16	17	18	19	20
21	22	23	24	25	26	27
28	29	30	31			

PRODUCED BY GALLERY A.P.J. graphic station phone 03-3904-3561

© 2002 The LEGO Group

WEDNESDAY
NEW YEAR'S DAY

1 January

© 2002 The LEGO Group

FRIDAY
ST. VALENTINE'S DAY

2 February

© 2002 The LEGO Group

TUESDAY

3 March

© 2002 The LEGO Group

THURSDAY

4 April

© 2002 The LEGO Group

SUNDAY
MOTHER'S DAY

5 May

LEGOLAND® DEUTSCHLAND

May 17th 2002, the 4th LEGOLAND in the
world was opened in Deutschland, Germany.
The size of this LEGOLAND is 485,605m².
Fly to visit there !

LEGO FACTS

LEGO® 日めくりカレンダー 2003 LEGO® DAILY CALENDAR 2003 JAPAN
プロパティビジネス Properties business
CL: ソニー・クリエイティブプロダクツ Sony Creative Products Inc. CD, AD, D, I: 芦野紀子 Noriko Ashino D: 熊野 由 Yuki Kumano I: 北川麻衣子 Maiko Kitagawa
DF, S: ソニー・クリエイティブプロダクツ Sony Creative Products Inc. DF: モアロッカーズ MORE ROCKERS

© 2002 The LEGO Group

MONDAY

STAR FESTIVAL

7 July

© 2002 The LEGO Group

WEDNESDAY

8 August

© 2002 The LEGO Group

TUESDAY

AUTUMNAL EQUINOX DAY

9 September

© 2002 The LEGO Group

FRIDAY

HALLOWEEN

10 October

© 2002 The LEGO Group

SATURDAY

11 November

© 2002 The LEGO Group

WEDNESDAY

NEW YEAR'S EVE

12 December

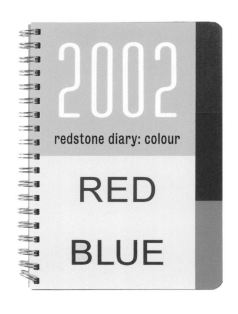

2002
redstone diary: colour

RED
BLUE

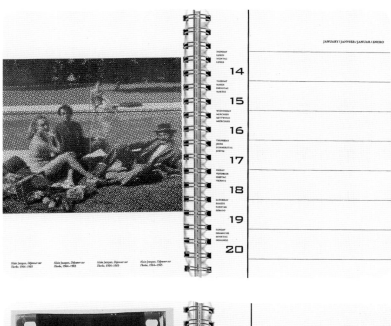

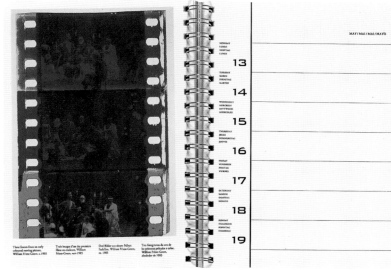

THE REDSTONE DIARY 2002　U.K

出版　Publisher
CL: Redstone Press　D: Julian Rothenstein　S: Redstone Press

THE REDSTONE DIARY 2003   U.K

出版 Publisher
CL: Redstone Press   D: Julian Rothenstein   S: Redstone Press

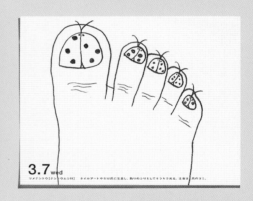

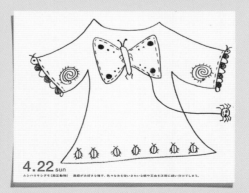

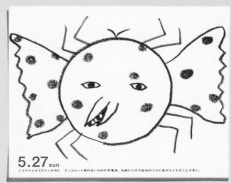

365ひきの誕生虫　365 BIRTHDAY INSECTS　2001　JAPAN

出版　Publisher
CL: パルコ出版　PARCO　CD: 佐倉康彦　Yasuhiko Sakura　AD, I: 野田　凪　Nagi Noda　CW: 本多若菜　Wakana Honda　DF, S: サン・アド　SUN-AD CO.,LTD.

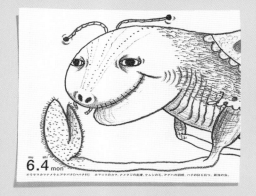

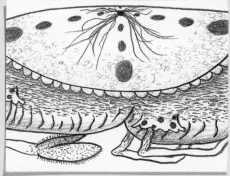

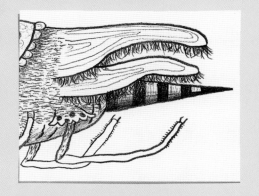

6.5 tue

8.10 fri

10.17 wed

10.25 thu

11.18 sun

12.25 tue

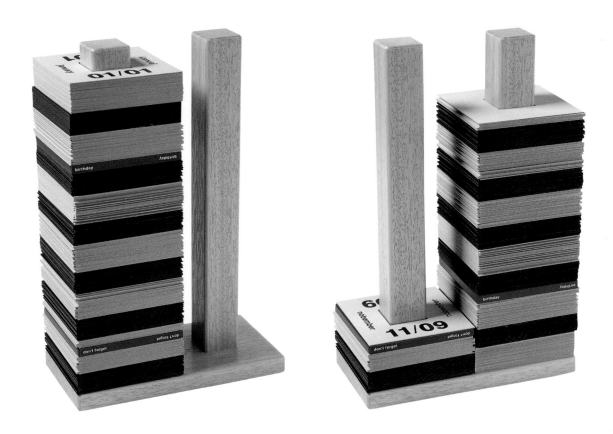

ブロックカレンダー　**Block Calendar**　Perpetual Calendar　JAPAN
家具インテリア用品及び生活雑貨の小売　Retail of furniture interior goods & life miscellaneous goods
CL: バルス　BALS CORPORATION　AD: 水野　学　Manabu Mizuno　D: 原田幸子　Sachiko Harada　I: Sachi　DF, S: グッドデザインカンパニー　good design company

day／365　Perpetual Calendar　JAPAN
洋紙販売・輸出入、物流機械器具システムの販売　Sales & Trading of paper. Sales of warehouse rack system & the related tools
CL: 竹尾　Takeo Company Limited　AD: 松下　計　Kei Matsushita　D: 田辺智子　Tomoko Tanabe　S: 松下計デザイン室　Kei Matsushita Design Room Inc.

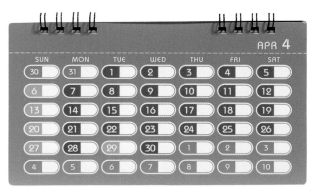

サプリメント　SUPPLEMENT　2003　JAPAN

ギフトラッピング及びファッショングッズの企画販売　Manufacture & Whole saler for gift wrapping products
CL: ゾナルトアンドカンパニー　ZONART & CO.,LTD.　CD: 木村　勝　Katsu Kimura　AD: 中島千鶴　Chizuru Nakajima　D: 大森英司　Eiji Ohmori
DF: パッケージングディレクション　Katsu Kimura & Packaging Direction CO.,LTD.　S: ゾナルトアンドカンパニー　ZONART & CO.,LTD.

インデックス　INDEX　2003　JAPAN

ギフトラッピング及びファッショングッズの企画販売　Manufacture & Whole saler for gift wrapping products
CL: ゾナルトアンドカンパニー　ZONART & CO.,LTD.　CD: 木村　勝　Katsu Kimura　AD: 中島千鶴　Chizuru Nakajima　D: 中村あい　Ai Nakamura
DF: パッケージングディレクション　Katsu Kimura & Packaging Direction CO.,LTD.　S: ゾナルトアンドカンパニー　ZONART & CO.,LTD.

鼻兎カレンダー Hana-Usagi Calendar 2002 JAPAN

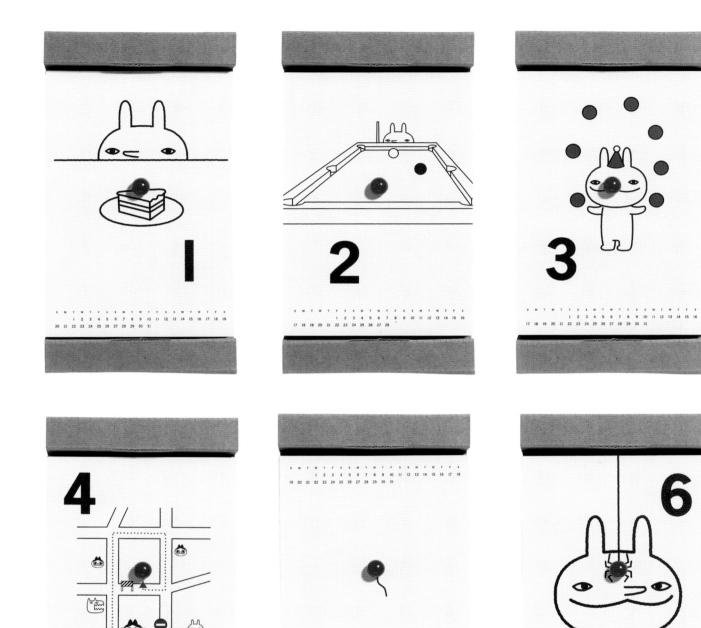

鼻兎カレンダー Hana-Usagi Calendar 2002 JAPAN
出版 Publisher
CL: 講談社 Kodansha Ltd.   AD: 水野　学 Manabu Mizuno   D: 高橋　剛 Go Takahashi   DF, S: グッドデザインカンパニー good design company
12ヶ月分のバラバラなカレンダーを赤いプッシュピンで留めている　A 12-month calendar composed of loose pages fastened with a red push-pin.

雑貨の製造・販売
CL: フェリシモ　FELISSIMO CORPORATION

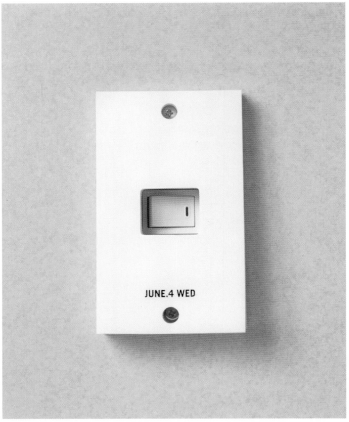

SWITCH PLATE CALENDAR　2003　JAPAN

雑貨の製造・販売　Manufacture & Sales of miscellaneous goods
CL: フェリシモ　FELISSIMO CORPORATION　AD: 石井洋二　Yoji Ishii : 野田　凪　Nagi Noda　D: 引地摩里子　Mariko Hikichi　DF, S: サン・アド　SUN-AD CO.,LTD.

日めくりカレンダーとスイッチパネルを兼ねたカレンダー　A daily calendar that doubles as a switch plate.

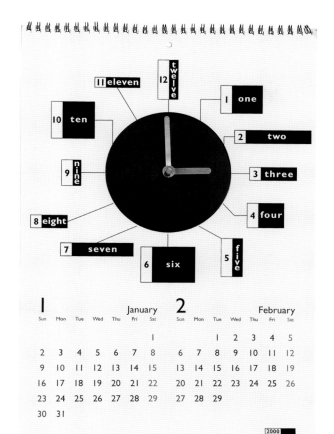

1				January				2				February			
Sun	Mon	Tue	Wed	Thu	Fri	Sat		Sun	Mon	Tue	Wed	Thu	Fri	Sat	
						1				1	2	3	4	5	
2	3	4	5	6	7	8		6	7	8	9	10	11	12	
9	10	11	12	13	14	15		13	14	15	16	17	18	19	
16	17	18	19	20	21	22		20	21	22	23	24	25	26	
23	24	25	26	27	28	29		27	28	29					
30	31														

2000

3				March				4				April			
Sun	Mon	Tue	Wed	Thu	Fri	Sat		Sun	Mon	Tue	Wed	Thu	Fri	Sat	
		1	2	3	4									1	
5	6	7	8	9	10	11		2	3	4	5	6	7	8	
12	13	14	15	16	17	18		9	10	11	12	13	14	15	
19	20	21	22	23	24	25		16	17	18	19	20	21	22	
26	27	28	29	30	31			23	24	25	26	27	28	29	
								30							

2000

9				September				10				October			
Sun	Mon	Tue	Wed	Thu	Fri	Sat		Sun	Mon	Tue	Wed	Thu	Fri	Sat	
					1	2		1	2	3	4	5	6	7	
3	4	5	6	7	8	9		8	9	10	11	12	13	14	
10	11	12	13	14	15	16		15	16	17	18	19	20	21	
17	18	19	20	21	22	23		22	23	24	25	26	27	28	
24	25	26	27	28	29	30		29	30	31					

2000

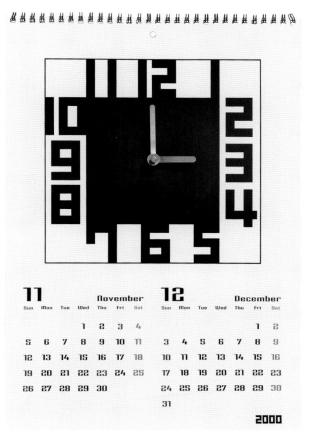

11				November				12				December			
Sun	Mon	Tue	Wed	Thu	Fri	Sat		Sun	Mon	Tue	Wed	Thu	Fri	Sat	
		1	2	3	4								1	2	
5	6	7	8	9	10	11		3	4	5	6	7	8	9	
12	13	14	15	16	17	18		10	11	12	13	14	15	16	
19	20	21	22	23	24	25		17	18	19	20	21	22	23	
26	27	28	29	30				24	25	26	27	28	29	30	
								31							

2000

CLOCKS　クロックス　2000　JAPAN
雑貨の企画、印刷　Goods planning & Printing
CL: プラルト　PRART CO.,LTD.　AD, D, S: 白川由美　Yumi Shirakawa

レコードカレンダー Record Calendar 2003 JAPAN
イラストレーター Illustrator
CL: 中谷麗菜 Rena Nakatani　Artist: 中谷麗菜 Rena Nakatani　S: アートハウス ART HOUSE

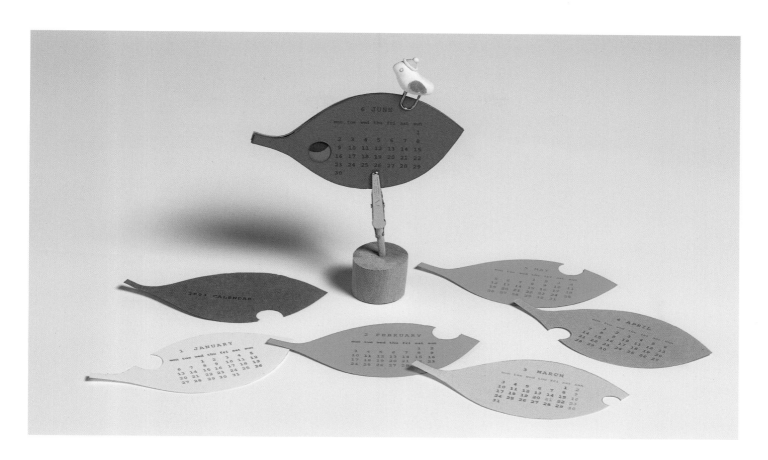

はっぱカレンダー　Leaf Calendar　2003　JAPAN
造形作家　Plastic artist
CL: 酒巻　恵　Megumi Sakamaki　Artist: 酒巻　恵　Megumi Sakamaki　S: アートハウス　ART HOUSE

ひつじちゃん とんがりカレンダー　Sheep Calendar　2003　JAPAN
造形作家　Plastic artist
CL: 酒巻　恵　Megumi Sakamaki　Artist: 酒巻　恵　Megumi Sakamaki　S: アートハウス　ART HOUSE

vegetables & fruits CUBE　2003　JAPAN
イラストレーター　Illustrator
CL: ハラダ マサミ　Masami Harada　Artist: ハラダ マサミ　Masami Harada　S: アートハウス　ART HOUSE

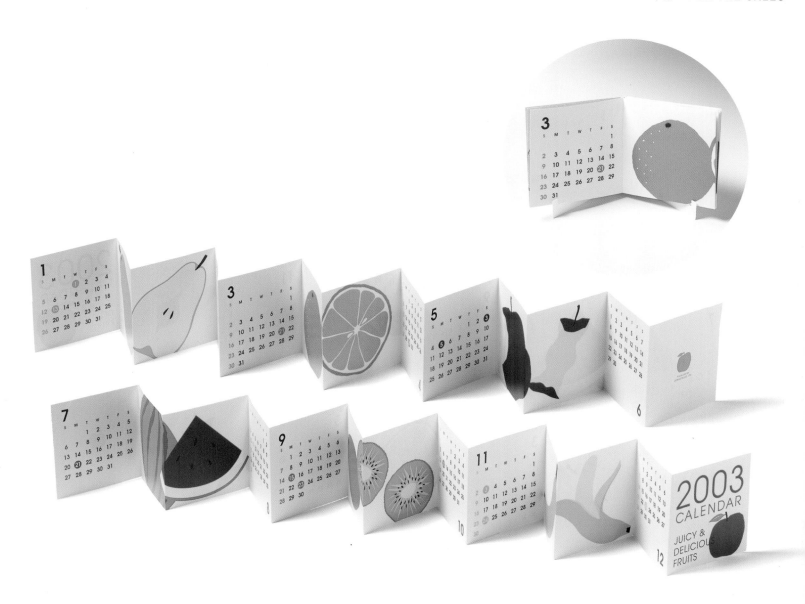

フルーツ FRUITS 2003 JAPAN

ギフトラッピング及びファッショングッズの企画販売 Manufacture & Whole saler for gift wrapping products
CL: ゾナルトアンドカンパニー ZONART & CO.,LTD. CD: 木村 勝 Katsu Kimura AD: 中島千鶴 Chizuru Nakajima D, I: 中村あい Ai Nakamura
DF: パッケージングディレクション Katsu Kimura & Packaging Direction CO.,LTD. S: ゾナルトアンドカンパニー ZONART & CO.,LTD.

カラーレリーフ COLOR RELIEF 2003 JAPAN

ギフトラッピング及びファッショングッズの企画販売 Manufacture & Whole saler for gift wrapping products
CL: ゾナルトアンドカンパニー ZONART & CO.,LTD. CD: 木村 勝 Katsu Kimura AD: 中島千鶴 Chizuru Nakajima D, I: 大森英司 Eiji Ohmori
DF: パッケージングディレクション Katsu Kimura & Packaging Direction CO.,LTD. S: ゾナルトアンドカンパニー ZONART & CO.,LTD.

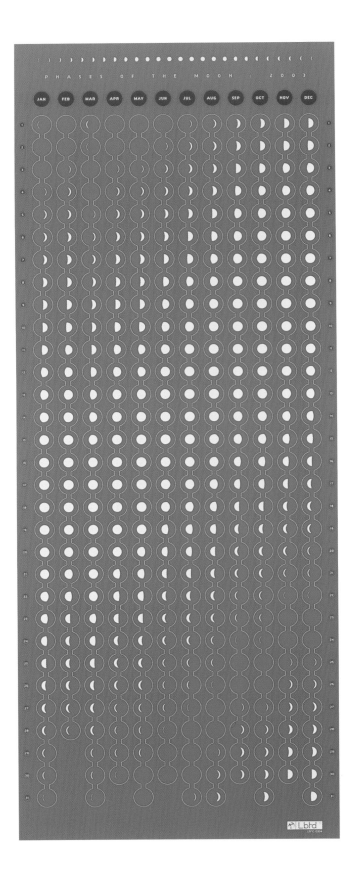

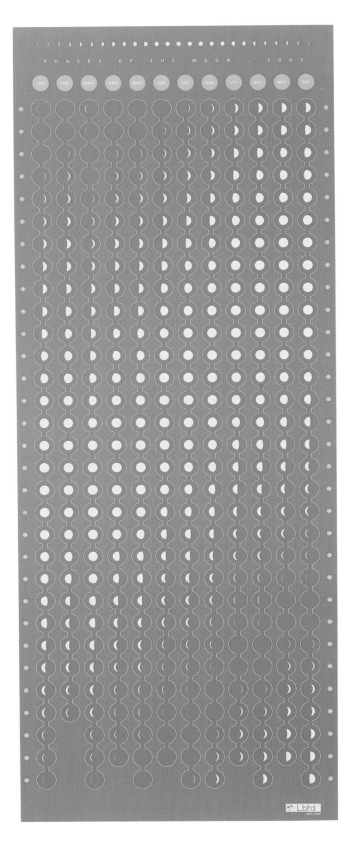

Phases of the Moon　2003　JAPAN

デザイン及びプロダクト制作　Design & Product production
CL: 野方電機工業 デザインプロダクト部 Nogata Denki Kogyo Co.,Ltd.　CD, D: 狩野潤哉　Junya Kano　S: Creative Resource Institute Inc.

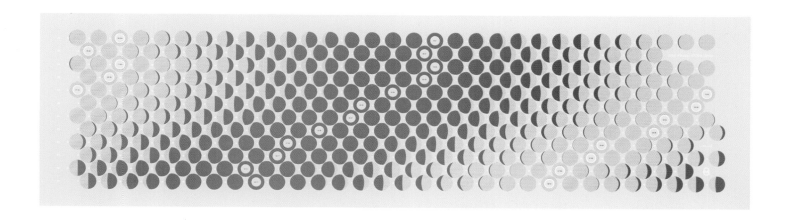

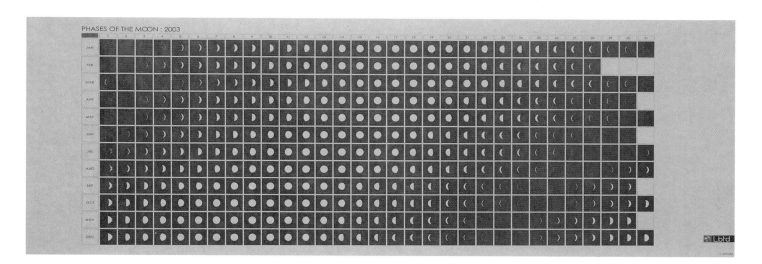

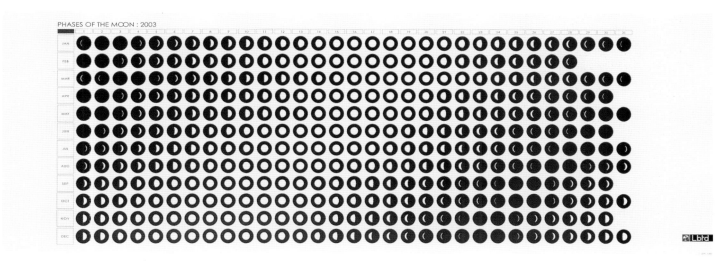

Phases of the Moon　2003　JAPAN

デザイン及びプロダクト制作　Design & Product production
CL: 野方電機工業 デザインプロダクト部　Nogata Denki Kogyo Co.,Ltd.　CD, D: 石崎　塁　Lui Ishizaki　S: Creative Resource Institute Inc.

Phases of the Moon　2003　JAPAN

デザイン及びプロダクト制作　Design & Product production
CL: 野方電機工業 デザインプロダクト部　Nogata Denki Kogyo Co.,Ltd.　CD, D: 狩野潤哉　Junya Kano　S: Creative Resource Institute Inc.

January, 2003

Sunday	Monday	Tuesday	Wednesday	Thursday	Friday	Saturday
			1	2	3	4
5	6	7	8	9	10	11
12	13	14	15	16	17	18
19	20	21	22	23	24	25
26	27	28	29	30	31	

December, 2003

January, 2004

S	M	T	W	T	F	S
				1	2	3
4	5	6	7	8	9	10
11	12	13	14	15	16	17
18	19	20	21	22	23	24
25	26	27	28	29	30	31

Sunday	Monday	Tuesday	Wednesday	Thursday	Friday	Saturday
	1	2	3	4	5	6
7	8	9	10	11	12	13
14	15	16	17	18	19	20
21	22	23	24	25	26	27
28	29	30	31			

2003 CALENDAR JAPAN
ギャラリー Gallery
CL: アンドーギャラリー ANDO GALLERY,INC. Producer: 安東孝一 Koichi Ando : 徳永あかね Akane Tokunaga AD: 葛西 薫 Kaoru Kasai D: 池田泰幸 Yasuyuki Ikeda DF, S: サン・アド SUN-AD CO.,LTD.

CALENDAR CUBE 2003　JAPAN

点字印刷　Braille printing
CL: ブレイルコム　brailleccm co.,ltd.　AD, D: 髙橋正実　Masami Takahashi　DF, S: マサミデザイン　MASAMI DESIGN

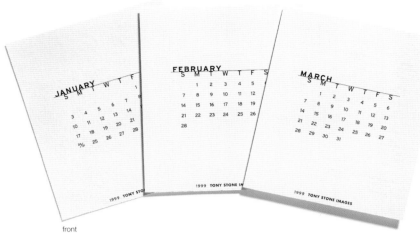

front

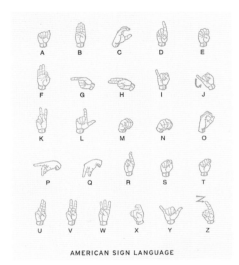

AMERICAN SIGN LANGUAGE

INTERNATIONAL MORSE CODE

TRAVEL SYMBOLS

EMOTICONS

ENGLISH BRAILLE ALPHABET

SEMAPHORE FLAG SIGNALS

back

CAN WE TALK?　1999　U.S.A
ストックフォト　Stock photo
CL: TONY STONE IMAGES　AD, D: Carlos Segura　S: SEGURA INC.

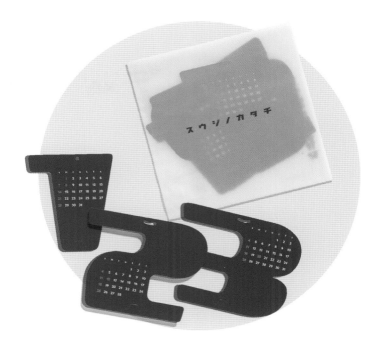

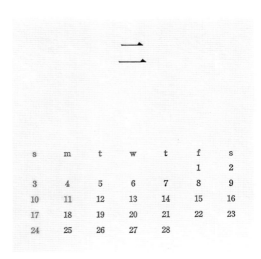

	s	m	t	w	t	f	s
二							
						1	2
	3	4	5	6	7	8	9
	10	11	12	13	14	15	16
	17	18	19	20	21	22	23
	24	25	26	27	28		

	s	m	t	w	t	f	s
七		1	2	3	4	5	6
	7	8	9	10	11	12	13
	14	15	16	17	18	19	20
	21	22	23	24	25	26	27
	28	29	30	31			

スウジノカタチ the shape of numbers 2001 JAPAN
広告・SP・パッケージの企画・制作 AD, SP, Package-design
CL: 第一紙行 DAIICHISHIKO CO.,LTD. CD, D, S: 藤田祐子 Yuko Fujita DF: 第一紙行 DAIICHISHIKO CO.,LTD.

活版タイポ Kappan-Typo 2002 JAPAN
広告・SP・パッケージの企画・制作 AD, SP, Package-design
CL: 第一紙行 DAIICHISHIKO CO.,LTD. CD, CW: 正井彩香 Ayaka Masai AD, D, S: 橋本 隆 Takashi Hashimoto DF: 第一紙行 DAIICHISHIKO CO.,LTD.

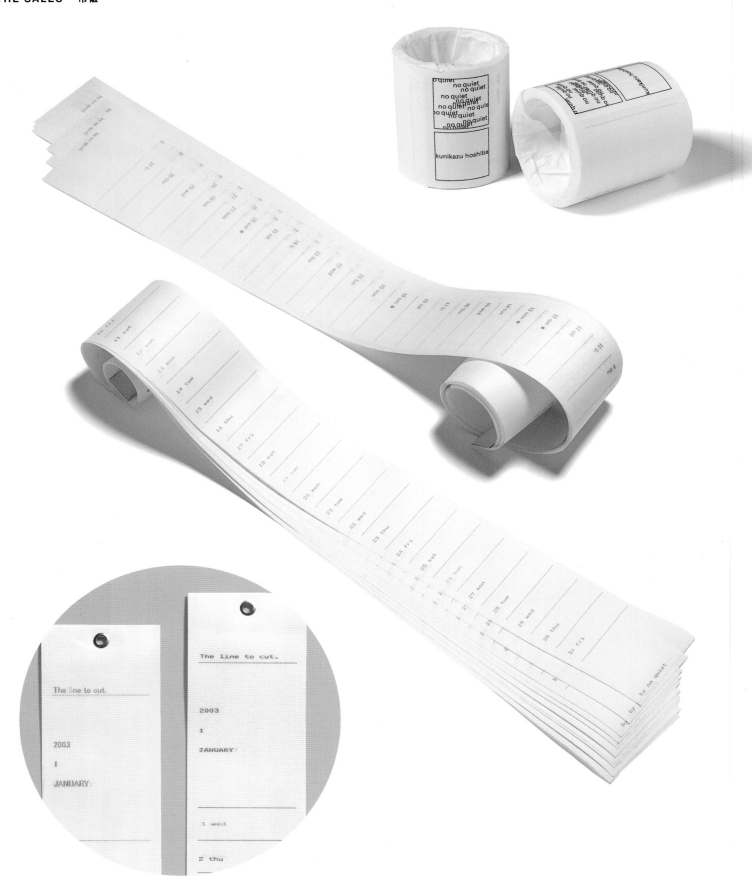

レシート・カレンダー receipt calendar 2003 JAPAN
プランニング、デザイン、セールス Design works
CL: カタチ katachi D: 干場邦一 Kunikazu Hoshiba S: カタチ katachi

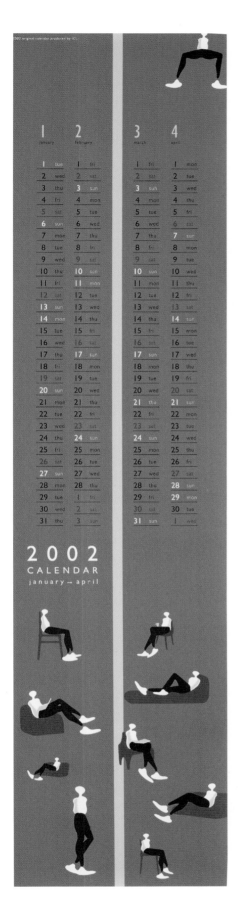

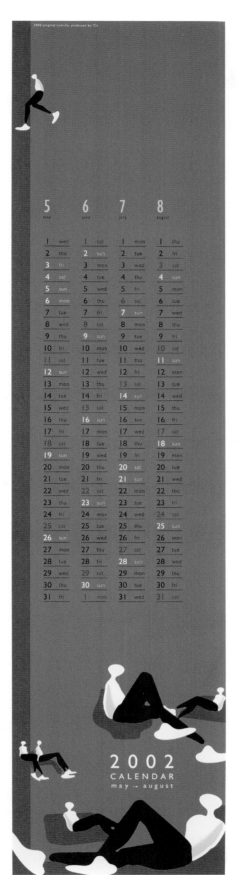

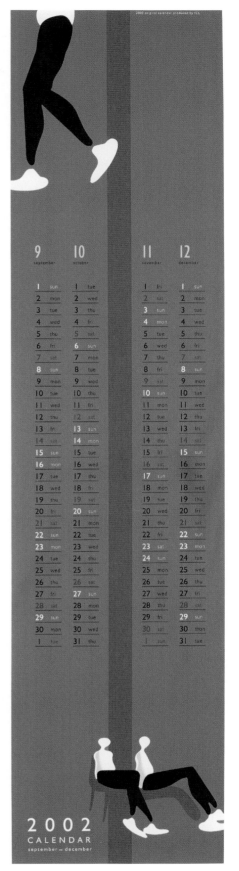

ICL 2002 "yururuca" CALENDAR JAPAN
ファッション・雑貨の企画販売と飲食店の経営 Planning & Sales of fashion, miscellaneous goods. Management of restaurants
CL: SAZABY Inc.　CD, S: SAZABY Inc.　D: 松下 計 KEI Matsushita

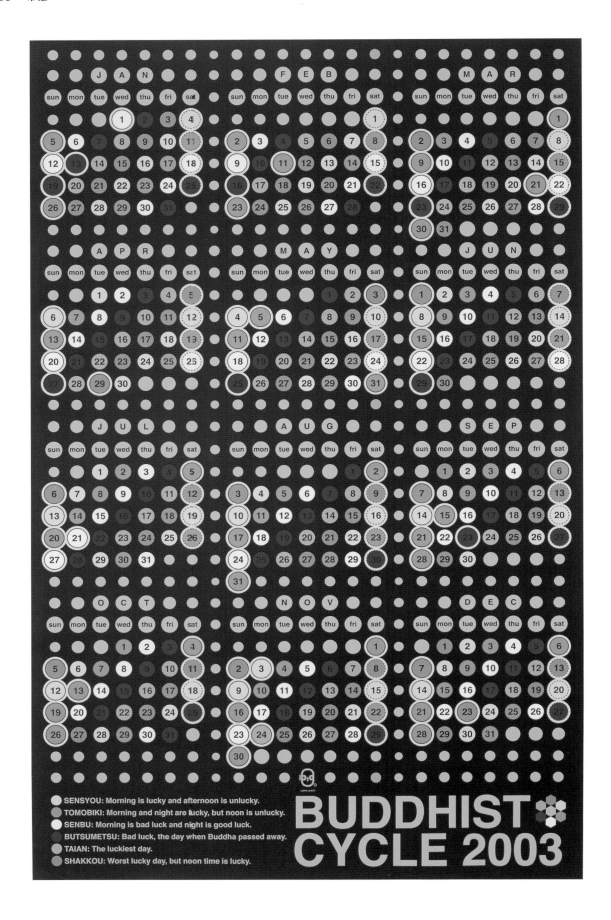

BUDDHIST CYCLE　2003 JAPAN

デザイン及びプロダクト制作　Design & Product production
CL: 野方電機工業 デザインプロダクト部　Nogata Denki Kogyo Co.,Ltd.　CD, D: 石崎　塁　Lui Ishizaki　S: Creative Resource Institute Inc.

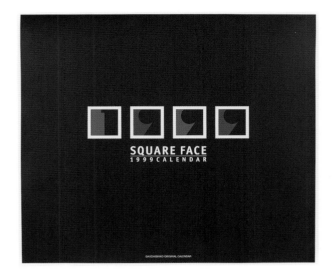

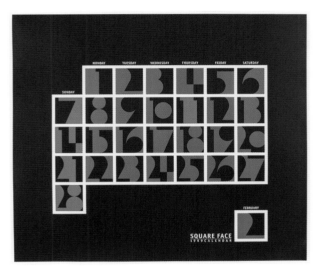

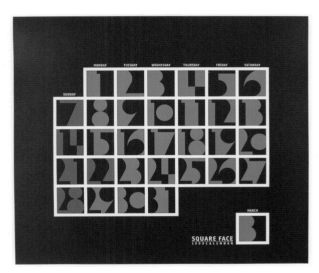

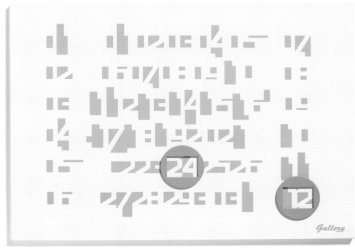

SQUARE FACE　1999　JAPAN
広告・SP・パッケージの企画・制作　AD, SP, Package-design
CL: 第一紙行　DAIICHISHIKO CO.,LTD.　CD, AD, D, S, Typo Designer: 橋本　隆　Takashi Hashimoto　DF: 第一紙行　DAIICHISHIKO CO.,LTD.

オリジナルカレンダー　Original Calendar　　Perpetual Calendar　JAPAN
インテリア・雑貨・アパレルのセレクト・ショップ　Selection shop of interior, miscellaneous goods & apparel
CL: ギャラリー1950　Gallery 1950　S: ギャラリー1950　Gallery 1950

月を左右に、日付を中央に配置。マグネットを貼ることで数字が見える仕組み　　The date flanked by images of the moon; a magnet is used to make the numbers appeared.

DAYLIGHT　デイライト　2003　JAPAN
メーカー、広告制作　Maker & Advertising
CL: D-BROS　CD: 宮田　識　Satoru Miyata　AD, D, P: 植原亮輔　Ryosuke Uehara　Producer: 中岡美奈子　Minako Nakaoka　DF: ドラフト　DRAFT co.,ltd.　S: D-BROS

1.-JANUARY   2002

SUNDAY	MONDAY	TUESDAY	WEDNESDAY	THURSDAY	FRIDAY	SATURDAY
		1	2	3	4	5
6	7	8	9	10	11	12
13	14	15	16	17	18	19
20	21	22	23	24	25	26
27	28	29	30	31		

JANUARY JANUAR JANVIER ENERO GENNAIO
1
2002

SUNDAY SONNTAG DIMANCHE DOMINGO DOMENICA	MONDAY MONTAG LUNDI LUNES LUNEDI	TUESDAY DIENSTAG MARDI MARTES MARTEDI	WEDNESDAY MITTWOCH MERCREDI MIÉRCOLES MERCOLEDI	THURSDAY DONNERSTAG JEUDI JUEVES GIOVEDI	FRIDAY FREITAG VENDREDI VIERNES VENERDI	SATURDAY SAMSTAG SAMEDI SÁBADO SABATO
30	31	1	2	3	4	5
6	7	8	9	10	11	12
13	14	15	16	17	18	19
20	21	22	23	24	25	26
27	28	29	30	31	1	2

2002 CALENDAR　JAPAN
出版　Publisher
CL: 創日社　SOBI CALENDARS CO.,LTD.　　CD, AD, D: 内田靖通　Yasumichi Uchida　　D: 小日向　誠　Makoto Obinata　　S: 凸版印刷　TOPPAN PRINTING CO.,LTD.

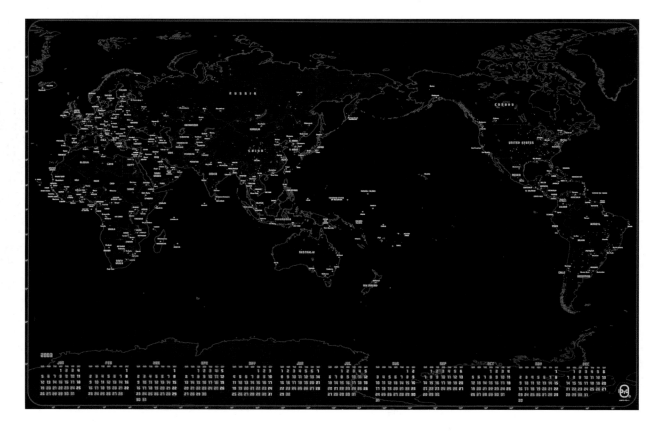

I'm a wanderer (Civilization & Ruins)　2003　JAPAN
デザイン及びプロダクト制作　Design & Product production
CL: 野方電機工業 デザインプロダクト部　Nogata Denki Kogyo Co.,Ltd.　CD, D: 狩野潤哉　Junya Kano　S: Creative Resource Institute Inc.

Night Planet & 2003 Calendar　JAPAN
デザイン及びプロダクト制作　Design & Product production
CL: 野方電機工業 デザインプロダクト部　Nogata Denki Kogyo Co.,Ltd.　CD, D: 石崎　塁　Lui Ishizaki　S: Creative Resource Institute Inc.

Index

CLIENTS

SUBMITTORS

new CALENDAR graphics

ニューカレンダー グラフィックス

Designer

柴 亜季子

Akiko Shiba

Editor

山本章子

Akiko Yamamoto

Writer

塚本朋子

Tomoko Tsukamoto

Photographer

藤本邦治

Kuniharu Fujimoto

Translator

パメラ・ミキ

Pamela Miki

Publisher

三芳伸吾

Shingo Miyoshi

2003年05月08日　初版第1刷発行

発行所　ピエ・ブックス
〒170-0005　東京都豊島区南大塚2-32-4
編集　Tel:03-5395-4820　Fax:03-5395-4821
e-mail:editor@piebooks.com
営業　Tel:03-5395-4811　Fax:03-5395-4812
e-mail:sales@piebooks.com

印刷・製本
大日本印刷(株)

©2003 PIE BOOKS

ISBN4-89444-257-4 C3070

Printed in Japan

SEASONAL/EVENT/SALES POSTCARD DESIGN
季節案内／イベント案内／セール案内のポストカードデザイン

Pages: 192 (Full Color)　各¥9,800+Tax

季節案内編は年賀状・暑中見舞・クリスマスカード
の特集。イベント案内編は企業の記念イベントや展
示会・映画の試写会・個人の結婚式・誕生・引越しの案
内状・企業の新商品案内の特集です。

The "Seasonal" collection focuses on New Year's,
Mid-summer, Christmas and other season's
greetings. The "Event" collection on announcements
for company anniversaries, exhibitions, film
showings, and private milestones such as marriages,
births, and address changes. The "Sales" collection
features a variety of new product, sale, and other
promotional postcards.

NEW BUSINESS CARD GRAPHICS Vol. 2
ニュー ビジネスカード グラフィックス 2

Pages: 224 (Full Color)　¥12,000+Tax

デザイナーや企業の名刺から、飲食店や販売店のシ
ョップカードまで、幅広い業種の優れた作品約850
点を、シンプルでシックなデザインからポップでハ
イパーなデザインまで、4つのタイプ別に紹介。アイ
デア満載の1冊です。

A new and even more comprehensive volume of our
popular business card series. More than 850
selections, ranging from designers' personal name
cards and corporate business cards to restaurant
and retail shop cards. The cards are categorized by
genre: simple, chic, pop, and hyper.

TYPOGRAPHIC COMPOSITION: TEXT & TABLE LAYOUT DESIGN
タイポグラフィック コンポジション: 目次から本文のレイアウトまで

Pages: 224 (Full Color)　¥13,000+Tax

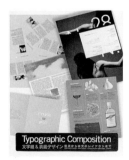

本書は、会社案内、カタログ、雑誌、書籍といった
多様な媒体の中で展開される優れた文字組・表組の
レイアウトを、『目次』、『テキストが多い場合の文字
組』、『ビジュアル中心の文字組』、『表組』の4つのカ
テゴリーに分類しています。

This volume present the some of the finest examples
of typographic composition from a variety of print
media-including company profiles, catalogs,
magazines, and books-grouped in four basic
categories: table of contents pages, primarily text
pages, captions/supplementary text on primarily
visual pages, and tables.

SHOP IMAGE GRAPHICS
ショップ イメージ グラフィックス

Pages: 240 (Full Color)　¥14,000+Tax

「グラフィックが個性的！」「空間デザインが魅力的！」
という視点で選び抜いたショップ約160店を衣食住
に分類して紹介。店舗の内外装写真と紙袋、カタロ
グ、メニューなどのグラフィックツールをショップ
別に掲載した貴重な1冊。

A special collection of over 160 shops selected for
their unique, individualistic graphics and appealing
interiors. This valuable volume presents
photographic documentation of each store interior
together with their most representative graphic
applications, including shopping bags, catalogs and
menus, categorized loosely under food, clothes, and
shelter.

CORPORATE PROFILE GRAPHICS Vol. 3
コーポレイト プロファイル グラフィックス 3

Pages: 224 (Full Color)　¥13,500+Tax

世界各国から集まった最新の会社・学校・施設案内
カタログから、デザインの質の高い作品ばかり約
200点を業種別に分類。構成、コンセプト、レイア
ウトを十分に堪能できるように、カバーから中ペー
ジまで見やすく紹介しています。

The latest catalogs of companies, schools, and
institutions from around the world, categorized by
specialty. Covers and selected inside pages from 200
high-quality catalogs are presented side-by-side to
help make their underlying concepts and layouts
more readily visible.

LIMITED RESOURCES/LIMITLESS CREATIVITY
限られた予算 VS 自由な発想 グラフィックス

Pages: 208(Full Color)　¥13,500+Tax

低予算でかつインパクトのある広告物、自然素材を
生かしたパッケージ、個性的で楽しい仕掛けのある
案内状や招待状の数々など約200作品を、そのデザ
インコンセプトと共に掲載。1ページめくるたびに
新しいアイデアに出会える1冊です。

A collection of works based on ideas that turn
limitations into creative advantages. Low
budget/high impact promotional pieces, packaging
that brings out the best of natural materials, highly
individual playfully devised announcements and
invitations—more than 200 unique works presented
with their design objectives. The ideas on each page
of this volume are as innovative as the next.

CATALOG + WEB GRAPHICS
カタログ+ WEB グラフィックス

Pages: 304 (Full Color)　¥15,000+Tax

販売促進を目的としたカタログ & パンフレットと、
そのホームページのデザインを衣食住の商品別に分
類し約70作品を紹介。優れたデザインのカタログ &
ホームページを、様式の違いが比較・一覧できるよ
うに同紙面上に掲載しています。

Exceptional catalog and website design compiled in
one volume! A collection of over 70 catalogs,
pamphlets and corresponding webpages designed to
promote sales, categorized by their products'
relation to the subjects "food, clothes, and shelter."
Both print and web pages are presented on the same
spread to facilitate comparison of how these superb
designs translate in the different mediums.

JAPANESE STYLE GRAPHICS
ジャパン スタイル グラフィックス

Pages: 224 (Full Color)　¥15,000+Tax

現代の日本人クリエイターたちが「和風」にこだわ
り、日本を感じさせる素材（文様、イラスト、写真、
色彩など）を取り入れてデザインした作品、日本の
文字が持つ形の美しさや文字組みにこだわった作品
を、アイテム別に紹介しています。

A graphic design collection that focuses on how
contemporary Japanese creators perceive and
express things Japanese. Outstanding graphic works
that consciously exploit Japanese aesthetics,
materials (including patterns, drawings, photographs, and color) and the unique characteristics
and beauty of the Japanese syllabaries as forms and
in composition.

ADVERTISING PHOTOGRAPHY IN JAPAN 2002

年鑑 日本の広告写真2002

Pages: 240 (Full Color) ¥14,500+Tax

気鋭の広告写真をそろえた（社）日本広告写真家協会（APA）の監修による本年鑑は、日本の広告界における最新のトレンドと、その証言者たる作品を一堂に見られる貴重な資料として、国内外の広告に携わる方にとって欠かせない存在です。

A spirited collection of works compiled under the editorial supervision of the Japan Advertising Photographers' Association (APA) representing the freshest talent in the Japanese advertising world. An indispensable reference for anyone concerned with advertising in or outside Japan.

NEW BUSINESS STATIONERY GRAPHICS

ニュー ビジネス ステーショナリー グラフィックス

Pages: 288 (Full Color) ¥14,000+Tax

レターヘッド、封筒、名刺は企業のイメージを伝える大切なツールです。機能的かつ洗練された作品からユニークで個性的な作品まで、世界22カ国のデザイナーから寄せられた作品から約450点を厳選し紹介します。好評の前作をより充実させた続編。

Letterheads, envelopes, and business cards are just a few of the essential business tools used to reinforce a company's image. More than 450 outstanding works—from the functional and refined to the unique and individualistic—by designers from 22 countries around the world. Even more substantial than our popular previous edition.

DIRECT MAIL ON TARGET

PR効果の高いDMデザイン

Pages: 224 (Full Color) ¥14,000+Tax

「送り手の思いを届ける」をコンセプトに、素材感を生かした作品、また封を切ったときの驚きや喜びを味わう作品など、イメージを消費者に訴えるダイレクトメールの数々を特集！新しく柔軟な発想が求められるDM制作にかかせない一冊です。

600 direct mail pieces designed to "deliver the intended message." This collection presents a wide variety of impression-making direct mailers that exploit the qualities of the materials they are made of, and surprise and delight their recipients upon opening. A must for anyone interested in creating new and uniquely conceived direct mail.

PRESENTATION GRAPHICS 2

プレゼンテーション グラフィックス 2

Pages: 224 (Full Color) ¥15,000+Tax

好評の前作をより充実させた続編。世界12カ国40名以上のクリエイターによるデザイン制作の発想からプレゼンテーション、完成までの特集。話題作品のアイデアスケッチをはじめ、今まで見ることのできなかった制作の裏側を紹介した貴重な1冊。

The sequel of our popular first edition. More than 40 creators from 12 countries illustrate the complete presentation process, from initial idea sketches to polished comps. This unique, invaluable book shows aspects of the design world that rarely reach public domain.

CHARACTER WORLD

キャラクター ワールド

Pages: 232 (Full Color) ¥14,000+Tax

企業、団体、商品、イベントなどのPRに使用されたイメージキャラクターとシンボルマークを特集。基本的に収録作品は広告、ノベルティグッズ、パッケージなどの使用例と、キャラクター・プロフィール、制作コンセプトもあわせて紹介しています。

A special collection of image characters and symbol marks designed for use as PR tools for companies, organizations, products, and events. In addition to advertisements, novelties, packaging, and other actual examples of their applications, the works showcased are accompanied by design objective descriptions and character profiles.

TRAVEL & LEISURE GRAPHICS 2

トラベル & レジャー グラフィックス 2

Pages: 224 (Full Color) ¥15,000+Tax

ホテル、旅館、観光地、交通機関からアミューズメント施設までのグラフィックス約350点を一挙掲載！！パンフレットを中心にポスター、DM、カードなど…現地へ行かなければ入手困難な作品も含め紹介。資料としてそろえておきたい1冊です！

A richly varied selection of 350 samples of travel and leisure guide graphics. The collection conveniently presents tour information, sightseeing guides, posters, promotional pamphlets from airline, railroad companies, hotels, inns, facilities, and more. Pick up this one-volume reference, and have it all at your fingertrips without having to leave your seat, let alone leave town!

TYPOGRAPHIC COMPOSITION IN JAPAN

日本の文字組・表組 デザイン

Pages: 224 (Full Color) ¥14,000+Tax

日本語はタテ組もヨコ組も可能であり、使用される文字も多様性に富んでいます。本書は会社案内、PR誌、カタログ、雑誌…などの媒体から優れた日本語の文字組・表組のレイアウトを目次、本文レイアウト、表組のカテゴリー別に紹介します。

Japanese can be composed horizontally or vertically, using a variety of characters and syllabaries. This book presents outstanding examples of Japanese typography and tabulated data from media such as company profiles, PR brochures, catalogs, and magazines, categorized as: Table of Contents, Main Text, and Tables.

PAPER IN DESIGN

ペーパー イン デザイン

Pages: 192 (Full Color) + Special reference material (paper samples) ¥16,000+Tax

DM、カタログをはじめ書籍の装丁、商品パッケージなど、紙素材を利用し個性的な効果を上げている数多くの作品をアイテムにこだわらず紹介。掲載作品で使われている紙見本も添付、紙のテクスチャーを実際に確かめることができる仕様です。

A special collection of graphic applications that exploit the role paper plays in design. This collection presents a wide range of applications—DM, catalogs, books, and product packaging, etc.—in which paper is used to achieve unique visual statements. Actual paper samples accompany each work to demonstrate their texture and tactile qualities.

PICTOGRAM AND ICON GRAPHICS

ピクトグラム & アイコン グラフィックス

Pages: 200 (160 in Color) ¥13,000+Tax

ミュージアムや空港の施設案内表示から雑誌やWEB
サイトのアイコンまで、業種別に分類し、実用例と
ともに紹介しています。ピクトグラムの意味や使用
用途などもあわせて紹介した、他に類をみないまさ
に永久保存版の1冊です。

The world's most outstanding pictograms and
applications. From pictographs seen in museums,
airports and other facility signage to icons used in
magazines and on the web, the examples are shown
isolated and in application with captions identifying
their meanings and uses. Categorized by industry for
easy reference, no other book of its kind is as
comprehensive—it is indeed a permanent archives in
one volume!

BUSINESS PUBLICATION STYLE

PR誌企画&デザイン 年間ケーススタディ

Pages: 224 (Full Color) ¥15,000+Tax

PR誌の年間企画スケジュールとビジュアル展開を1
年分まとめて紹介します。特集はどういう内容で構
成しているのか？エッセイの内容と執筆人は？など、
創刊・リニューアル時の企画段階から役立つ待望の
1冊です。

Year-long case studies of 40 critically selected PR
magazines.What should the content of the feature
stories composed ? What should the subject of the
essays be and who should write them? This eagerly
awaited collection promises to assist in the planning
stages for the inauguration or renewal of business
periodicals.

SMALL PAMPHLET GRAPHICS

スモール パンフレット グラフィックス

Pages: 224 (Full Color) ¥14,000+Tax

街や店頭で見かける様々な企業、ショップのパンフ
レットを衣・食・住・遊の業種別に紹介します。気
軽に持ち帰ることができる数多くの小型パンフレッ
トの中からデザイン性に優れた作品約300点を厳選
しました。

A collection introducing a wide variety of company
and shop pamphlets found in stores and around
town, grouped under the categories "food, clothes,
shelter, and entertainment." 300 small-scale
pamphlets selected for their outstanding design
qualities from the great many pieces available to
customers for the taking.

THE TOKYO TYPE DIRECTORS CLUB ANNUAL 2002

TDC年鑑 '02

Pages: 252 (Full Color) ¥15,000+Tax

温故知新の精神を大切にしながら、更に新しい次世
代のタイポグラフィー＆タイポディレクション作品
を探究する国際グラフィックデザイン・コンペティ
ション「TDC」。インタラクティブ作品も拡充、より
幅広いメディアの優れた作品を紹介しています。

JTDC—the international graphic design competition that
investigates new generations of typography and type
direction in light of masterpieces from the past. With
the inclusion of interactive pieces in recent years, the 2002
annual presents outstanding works from an extensive
range of media.

MAIL ORDER GRAPHICS: Catalog + Web

通販カタログ＋WEB グラフィックス

Pages: 304 (Full Color) ¥15,000+Tax

世界各国の通販カタログと通販Webサイトの中から
デザイン、機能性に優れた作品を厳選。カタログと
Webサイトの両方を駆使し、大きな反響を得ている
数々の通販デザインを紹介しています。デザイナー
からの声も載せた貴重な一冊です。

Mail-order design that moves consumers and sells
products! This collection presents functionally and
visually outstanding examples of catalog and website
design, which working in tandem have created
sensations in the world of mail order. With
commentary by the designers, this volume forms a
valuable resource of catalog design—both in-print
and on-line.

NEW COMPANY BROCHURE DESIGN 2

ニュー カンパニー ブローシャー デザイン 2

Pages: 272 (Full Color) ¥15,000+Tax

デザインの優れた案内カタログ約150点とWEB約50
点を厳選。WEBサイトはカタログと連動した作品を
中心に紹介しています。また各作品の企画・構成内
容がわかるように制作コンセプト・コンテンツのキ
ャッチコピーを具体的に掲載しています。

A selection of over 150 superbly designed brochures
and 50 corresponding websites. All works are
accompanied by descriptions of their design
objectives and catch copy, to provide added insight
into their planning and compositional structures.

ONE & TWO COLOR GRAPHICS IN JAPAN

日本の1&2色 グラフィックス

Pages: 224 (Full Color) ¥15,000+Tax

2色までの刷色で効果的にデザインされた日本のグラ
フィック作品を、使用された刷色の色見本とDICナン
バーを紹介。グラデーションが効果的な作品やダブ
ルトーンの作品には、色のかけ合わせと濃度変化が
わかるカラー・チャートを併載しています。

A collection of Japanese graphics that are effectively
reproduced using only one or two ink colors.
Posters, flyers, direct mailers, packaging and more,
that have no less impact than their four-color
competition. Each work is presented together with
color swatches and the DIC numbers of their ink
colors used.

ENVIRONMENT/WELFARE-RELATED GRAPHICS

環境・福祉 グラフィックス

Pages: 240 (Full Color) ¥15,000+Tax

環境保全への配慮が世界的な常識となりつつある今
日、企業も積極的に環境・福祉など社会的テーマを
中心にした広告キャンペーンを展開しています。国
内外の優れた環境・福祉広告を紹介した本書は今後
の広告を考えるために必携の1冊となるでしょう。

Environmental conservation is now a worldwide
concern, and corporate advertising campaigns based
on environmental and social themes are on the rise.
This collection of noteworthy local and international
environment/welfare-related publicity is an essential
reference for anyone involved in the planning and
development of future advertising.

カタログ・新刊のご案内について

総合カタログ、新刊案内をご希望の方は、はさみ込みのアンケートはがきを
ご返送いただくか、90円切手同封の上、ピエ・ブックス宛お申し込みください。

CATALOGS and INFORMATION ON NEW PUBLICATIONS

If you would like to receive a free copy of our general catalog
or details of our new publications, please fill out the enclosed postcard
and return it to us by mail or fax.

CATALOGUES ET INFORMATIONS SUR LES NOUVELLES PUBLICATIONS

Si vous désirez recevoir un exemplaire qratuit de notre catalogue généralou des
détails sur nos nouvelles publication. veuillez compléter la carte réponse incluse et
nous la retourner par courrierou par fax.

CATALOGE und INFORMATIONEN ÜBER NEUE TITLE

Wenn Sie unseren Gesamtkatalog oder Detailinformationen über
unsere neuen Titel wünschen.fullen Sie bitte die beigefügte Postkarte aus
und schicken Sie sie uns per Post oder Fax.

ピエ・ブックス

〒170-0005　東京都豊島区南大塚2-32-4
TEL: 03-5395-4811　FAX: 03-5395-4812
www.piebooks.com

PIE　BOOKS

2-32-4 Minami-Otsuka Toshima-ku Tokyo 170-0005　JAPAN
TEL：+81-3-5395-4811　FAX：+81-3-5395-4812
www.piebooks.com